GOD KEEPS HIS PROMISES

BY CURRY R. BLAKE

General Overseer

John G. Lake Ministries

and

Dominion Life

International Apostolic Church

TABLE OF CONTENTS

PREFACE

The very basis of our faith in God is that He keeps His Promises. Throughout scripture we see God making promises by way of prophetic words and other means. The fact that He has such a good "track record" (100% fulfillment), is why we can and should have a simple, solid, unshakeable faith in Him.

Many people often use the term "blind faith" in reference to trusting God to keep His word. We have the same standard for humans that we have for God. If you say something or promise something, you should keep your word and do what you promised. We trust people because they have proven they can be trusted. God has proven that He too can and should be trusted.

As you read this book, take time to meditate upon the teaching. Don't rush through it, take time to think about what is being said. This teaching is so fundamental and yet so profound in its simplicity and truth.

W W. Houwy Link

God Keeps His Promises

651 602   1880

Chapter 1

God Keeps His Promises

FAX# 390 ROBERTS N

651-602 1313

————◆——◈——◆————

Do you believe that God keeps His promises? Say this with me: "God keeps His promises!" Say it again; say it louder. "God Keeps His Promises!" Now, say it like you mean it. "GOD KEEPS HIS PROMISES!" Amen!

Let's look at the definition of the word *promise*: when used as a noun *it is a declaration or an assurance that one will do a particular thing or that a particular thing will happen.* Notice that this is a particular thing, not just a "well, anything could happen" thing. This is a particular thing when God says, "This will happen."

There are synonyms such as: *a word, giving your word, a word of honor, an assurance, a pledge, a vow, a guarantee, an oath, a bond, or a covenant.* According to the dictionary all of these are synonyms for the word, *promise.*

When *promise* is used as a verb, *it is for one person to assure another person that they will definitely do, give, or arrange for something to be done or to declare that something will happen.* The synonyms there are: *to swear, to pledge, to vow, to guarantee, to bind oneself, or to make covenant.* The second definition is *to give good grounds for expecting a particular occurrence or situation to happen.*

You may think, "Okay, that's a promise; I knew that." I just wanted to let you know the specifics; it is a specific declaration. In other words, if we're talking about man, that's one thing, but when we talk about God, that's something totally different. He specifically made particular promises, and He did that throughout the history of mankind.

2 Corinthians chapter 1, starting in verse 17, Paul says,

> *17 When I therefore was thus minded, did I use lightness? or the things that I purpose, do I purpose according to the flesh, that with me there should be yea yea, and nay nay?*

Paul didn't just flippantly say, "Oh, yea, yea, I'll do that," or "No, I'm not going to do that." No, he was saying, "I didn't say it in lightness. I didn't say it in passing. It wasn't a light thing. If I gave my yea, it was yea. If I gave my nay, it was nay." In other words it was either a yes or no. Paul said, "I'm a man of my word. I'm doing what I said I was going to do." He didn't use lightness; He didn't just flippantly say it.

18 But as God is true, our word toward you was not yea and nay.

It was either yes or no.

19 For the Son of God, Jesus Christ, who was preached among you by us, even by me and Silvanus and Timotheus, was not yea and nay, but in him was yea.

Notice here he says, "…but in Him was yea." It wasn't yea and/or nay, but in Him was yea.

If you go in and read this, go back about 10 verses and read through about 10 verses after that. Get the whole context. Don't just come in and hear a message. Go back home, study this out, dig it out, and make it yours. In other words, study it, and own it. Do the diligence so that the enemy can't come and take it away from you.

Mark 4:15,

15 And these are they by the way side, where the word is sown; but when they have heard, Satan cometh immediately, and taketh away the word that was sown in their hearts.

Satan tries to steal away the Word that was sown in your heart. Don't let him do that. Go back home, and study it. Let him know that you're not just sitting there with your hands out, waiting for me to put something into them. Let the devil know that you got hold of this, and it is yours, and he's not going to take it from you.

2 Corinthians 1:20,

> *20 For all the promises of God in him are yea, and in him Amen, unto the glory of God by us.*

It says, "For all…" "All the promises of God in Him," in Christ, "are yea, and in Him Amen." The word, *amen*, means *so be it.* "For all," not some, "the promises of God in Christ are yes, and in Christ so be it!"

I want you to get the impact of that. If you get hold of this message, I guarantee that your life will change. This is not preacher rhetoric. This is not, "You'll never be the same again." I'm not saying that. I'm telling you that if you get hold of this, your life will change. How will you know when your life has changed? You'll know when people's lives around you start to change. Until your life is changed, you can't affect people. However, once your life is changed, you will start affecting the people around you.

He says here, "All the promises of God in Him are yes, and in Christ Amen." This is so amazing! You're *in* Christ. If you're *in* Christ, the promises of God are *yes and so be it*.

Do you realize that there is a requirement you have to fulfill to have all of the promises of God, *yes and so be it,* in your life? The requirement is that you have to be *in* Him. This is not a matter of you attaining something; this is you being *in* Him. Once you're *in* Him, everything *in* Him is *yes and so be it*. It's not even a question of whether it is God's will. A promise of God is God's will. He can't promise something that's not His will, and He has made all of these promises.

How do you get these promises? You get *in* Him, and because you are *in* Him, you're in a state where all of His promises are *yes and so be it*. It's not even a question of, "I'm going to pray and see if God answers." No. If you're *in* Him and you have a promise of God, it will be answered!

People come to us from around the world for ministry. They want us to lay hands on them, they want us to pray for them, and that's good. The reason they come to us is because I have settled in myself that the reason God hears and answers is because I am *in* Christ. It's not based on my goodness, or what I've obtained, or how many hours I've prayed, or how many days I've fasted this week, or anything else. It has to do with whether I'm *in* Christ. It's not a matter of me trying to deserve it; it's a matter of me getting *in* Him where the blessings are and where the answers are. The answers are in Him.

Notice what it says: "For all the promises of God *in* Him (Christ) are yes, and *in* Him Amen (so be it)." Why? It says, "Unto the glory of God by us." You might think, "Well, God wouldn't answer me." Let me tell you why God's going to answer you: when He answers you, it will bring Him glory. He's not answering you because you're so special, or you're so good, or you dress right, act right, or talk right. That's not why He's answering you. He's answering you because these promises are *yes and so be it* in your life, and because it brings glory to God to be able to answer your prayers.

Forget you; get you off your mind. You have to realize that when you pray God is looking for a reason to answer your prayers, not for a reason not to! God is looking for a reason to answer your prayers, because He wants people to see Him glorified. One of the ways He is glorified is through answered prayer. Amen.

Think about how charged up you get when you pray and then your prayer is answered. You get so excited and say, "God heard my prayer! I prayed and this happened." Then you have to move that from an event to a lifestyle. That should be the normal thing.

John 11:41-42,

> *41 Then they took away the stone from the place where the dead was laid. And Jesus lifted up his eyes, and said, Father, I thank thee that thou hast heard me.*

> *42 And I knew that thou hearest me always: but because of the people which stand by I said it, that they may believe that thou hast sent me.*

Jesus was saying, "Father, I pray to You, and I know You always hear Me. I'm just praying around these people so they will know." Imagine telling God, "I am praying, and I'm saying this out loud. There is not a question about You hearing me, because I know You always hear me. I'm just saying this so these other people can hear me."

Mark 16:18,

> *18 They shall take up serpents; and if they drink any deadly thing, it shall not hurt them; they*

shall lay hands on the sick, and they shall recover.

Most of the time when I pray it is during a service. When I minister to the sick, I don't have to pray. The Bible says, "Lay hands on the sick, and they will recover." Generally, I only pray because that's what people expect.

Mark 11:22-24,

> *22 And Jesus answering saith unto them, Have faith in God.*

> *23 For verily I say unto you, That whosoever shall say unto this mountain, Be thou removed, and be thou cast into the sea; and shall not doubt in his heart, but shall believe that those things which he saith shall come to pass; he shall have whatsoever he saith.*

> *24 Therefore I say unto you, What things soever ye desire, when ye pray, believe that ye receive them, and ye shall have them.*

According to Jesus' words, if I believe that I will receive what I ask for, it will come to pass; I shall have it. These things aren't separate issues; all of these things have to be working together.

Remember what I just read in 2 Corinthians 1:20: "For all the promises of God *in* Him are yes, and *in* Him Amen (so be it), unto the glory of God by us." When it said, "…unto the glory of God by us," it was telling us that God gets glory by us, because what we do brings Him glory.

The secret behind the hyper-grace belief is that people get to the point where they're afraid of works. They don't do any works because they don't want it to look like they're trying to earn salvation.

That is why the devil is against us doing works. He knows that God wants to receive glory by us, by our deeds, and by our works. It has nothing to do with earning, deserving, or getting saved by works, but the enemy does not want you doing works, because the more you do for God (believing God, having faith toward God, or out of gratitude to God), the more glory God gets. The enemy is trying to work through religious means to try to get people to do nothing, because when people do nothing, God gets less glory. I will prove that to you.

John 14:12-15,

> *12 Verily, verily, I say unto you, He that believeth on me, the works that I do shall he do also; and*

greater works than these shall he do; because I go unto my Father.

Jesus said, "I say unto you, he that believeth on Me…" If you believe on Him, He's talking about you. He didn't make any qualification other than the person has to be a believer. He didn't say it to any one person, so this is an open-ended promise that you get to participate in. "He that believeth on me, the works that I do shall he do also; and greater works than these shall he do; because I go unto my Father."

It's not because of your fasting, praying, or anything else; it's because He went to the Father. You need to understand this. Notice what He was saying to you: "The works that I do shall you do also, and greater works than these shall you do." Now, that is a good, practical explanation of grace. The reason that you get to do greater works is because He went to the Father. That's grace wrapped up in a nutshell, right there.

It has nothing to do with how good and perfect you've been, how you've never made a mistake, or anything else. It has to do with the fact that He went to the Father. Because He went to the Father, you get to do the same works and greater works—that's grace. Grace gives you the ability to work. Amen.

Look at verse 13. This is tied right in with it.

> *13 And whatsoever ye shall ask in my name, that will I do, that the Father may be glorified in the Son.*

"And whatsoever…" How big of a word is whatsoever? It's big; it covers everything. "And whatsoever you shall ask in My name, that will I do." Why? He said, "So that the Father may be glorified in the Son."

I just brought this out because I want you to realize what I read before in 2 Corinthians 1:20: "All the promises of God in Him are yes, and in Him Amen (so be it), unto the glory of God by us." Jesus had already said in John 14:13 that the reason God would answer our prayers was so the Father could be glorified in the Son. Have you ever thought about how Jesus ever lives to make intercession for us? He's praying for us.

If you named any one individual who has ever lived in the history of the universe who really guarantees that when He prays He will get answers, you would say that it's Jesus. He's praying for you! What does that mean? His prayers get answered; whatsoever He is praying for you is going to happen. Amen?

What did Jesus pray? He prayed that we may be one with one another, one with the Father, and one with Him. Guess what? That prayer was answered. It was answered in the Spirit; we are now one with Him. It shall be answered in the sense that the Church is going to grow up and get away from all of the bickering and fighting because of the titles over the door and grow into one Body.

In verse 13 He told us, "Whatsoever you shall ask in My Name, that will I do, that the Father may be glorified in the Son."

14 If ye shall ask any thing in my name, I will do it.

15 If ye love me, keep my commandments.

"If ye shall ask any thing in My name…" He said it again. It was if He was saying, "I know it's hard for you to believe, but I'm telling you, 'If you shall ask any thing in My name, I will do it.'" Then He threw that monkey wrench in there, "If you love Me, keep my commandments."

2 Corinthians chapter 1:21-24,

21 Now he which stablisheth us with you in Christ, and hath anointed us, is God;

"Now He which establishes us with you *in* Christ..." Notice: Paul had just said in verse 20 of that chapter, "All the promises of God *in* Christ are yes, and *in* Christ *so be it*." Then he said in verse 21, "Now He which establishes us with you *in* Christ," he was still talking about the same thing. "and [He Who] hath (past tense) anointed us, is God." God did this. God established this. This wasn't your idea; this was God's idea. Amen.

> *22 Who hath also sealed us, and given the earnest of the Spirit in our hearts.*

"Who hath also sealed us, and given the earnest," or as some translations say, "Who has also sealed us, and given the down payment of the Spirit in our hearts."

> *23 Moreover I call God for a record upon my soul, that to spare you I came not as yet unto Corinth.*

Do you realize what Paul was saying here? He was saying, "With God as my witness, the reason I haven't come to Corinth yet is to spare you." Why? He knew that they were messed up. This was his third letter. I know it says 2 Corinthians, but this was the third letter that he had actually written to them.

Every letter had to do with major sin in the Church, major_problems going on, major division, and preferences. They were saying, "I like this preacher better than the other one. I'm going to listen to him; he says something different."

Paul knew all of that was going on and he said, "I really want to come and visit you. I really want to come and impart something to you, but you don't want me there right now. If I show up, it isn't going to be fun." Think about that.

That doesn't sound like the typical Gospel message that you hear, because he was going there to correct them. He was going there to rebuke, correct, give them instruction, and righteousness, all through the Word of God.

> *24 Not for that we have dominion over your faith, but are helpers of your joy: for by faith ye stand.*

Paul wanted them to get right so he could show up again and help them.

2 Corinthians 2:1-4,

> *1 But I determined this with myself, that I would not come again to you in heaviness.*

In other words, "The last time I was there, there was heaviness; there were things I had to fix. I have determined I'm not going to go back there with things the way they are. Get things right, so I can show up again."

> *2 For if I make you sorry, who is he then that maketh me glad, but the same which is made sorry by me?*

He was saying, "I want to have joy in you. I don't want to come there and be mean. I don't want to come there and have to fix everything. I want to come there and have a good time with you."

> *3 And I wrote this same unto you, lest, when I came, I should have sorrow from them of whom I ought to rejoice; having confidence in you all, that my joy is the joy of you all.*

> *4 For out of much affliction and anguish of heart I wrote unto you with many tears; not that ye should be grieved, but that ye might know the love which I have more abundantly unto you.*

In other words, "I don't want you to always see me coming at you just to gripe at you. I'm trying to get you to grow up into Christ. I want to show up and have fellowship with you."

Go with me to 2 Corinthians chapter 6. Remember, we're talking about how God keeps His promises.

2 Corinthians 6:14-18,

> *14 Be ye not unequally yoked together with unbelievers: for what fellowship hath righteousness with unrighteousness? and what communion hath light with darkness?*
>
> *15 And what concord hath Christ with Belial? or what part hath he that believeth with an infidel?*

Here he was showing how different Christians are from the world and how different they should be.

> *16 And what agreement hath the temple of God with idols? for ye are the temple of the living God; as God hath said, I will dwell in them, and walk in them; and I will be their God, and they shall be my people.*

We sing the song about how God lives in us, but do we really believe that? Some just think, "Well, He lives in me so that when I die, I can go to heaven." Is that it or is there another purpose that He has for us because of His indwelling in us? You need to realize what it means to have the Spirit of the Living God living *in* you and that your body is His temple.

God dwells within each of us so our bodies are the temple of the Holy Ghost, not a temple made with hands, but He actually dwells *in* us, in our bodies.

"For you are the temple of the living God; as God has said, 'I *will* dwell in them, and walk in them; and I *will* be their God, and they *shall* be my people.'"

If you went back to John, where we were earlier, He said, "Whatsoever you *shall* ask in My name that *will* I do." Look at the words *shall* and *will*. Look at the words in verse 16, "I *will* dwell in them, and walk in them; and I *will* be their God, and they *shall* be My people." Do you hear the words *will* and *shall*? There are no stronger words in the English language or from the Greek that the words were taken from. There's no stronger emphatic word that a human can utter other than the words *will* and *shall*.

> 17 *Wherefore come out from among them, and be ye separate, saith the Lord, and touch not the unclean thing; and I will receive you,*

It doesn't say, "I might," but "I *will*."

> 18 *And will be a Father unto you, and ye shall be my sons and daughters, saith the Lord Almighty.*

He said, "I *will* receive you, And *will* be a Father unto you, and you *shall* be My sons and daughters." Look at how many times the words *shall* and *will* are used.

2 Corinthians 7:1-4,

> *1 Having therefore these promises, dearly beloved, let us cleanse ourselves from all filthiness of the flesh and spirit, perfecting holiness in the fear of God.*

"Having therefore these promises…" You ask, "What promises?" I just read them to you in verse 17: "If you come out from among them, and touch not the unclean thing, I *will* receive you." If you do what He asks, He *will* be your Father. He *will* walk in you, He *will* talk in you, and He *will* dwell in you.

By cleansing ourselves, we *will* be the temple of the Living God. God *will* live in us, He *will* dwell in us, and He *will* walk in us. He *will* be our God, and we *will* be His people. "Having these promises, let us cleanse ourselves from all filthiness of the flesh and spirit, perfecting holiness in the fear of God."

If I were to teach on the filthiness of the flesh and the spirit, it would show how our spirit can be contaminated. There's a large group of Christianity that doesn't believe that. Even though they don't see it, right here we are told that we have to cleanse ourselves. It doesn't say that God is going to do it. It says, "Having these promises, let us cleanse ourselves from all filthiness of the flesh and the spirit."

2 Receive us; we have wronged no man, we have corrupted no man, we have defrauded no man.

3 I speak not this to condemn you: for I have said before, that ye are in our hearts to die and live with you.

4 Great is my boldness of speech toward you, great is my glorying of you: I am filled with comfort, I am exceeding joyful in all our tribulation.

In other words, "No matter what I'm going through, you're on my heart and mind. Because of that, I have joy. I know that you're going to grow up. You're *in* Christ. He's going to walk in you. You're going to cleanse yourself. I have faith in you that you're going to be who God has called you to be."

We are still talking about how God keeps His promises.

2 Peter 3:1-18,

1   This second epistle, beloved, I now write unto you; in both which I stir up your pure minds by way of remembrance:

In other words, Peter was saying, "I have sent you two letters, and in both letters I am endeavoring to stir up your pure minds by reminding you of some things."

> 2 *That ye may be mindful of the words which were spoken before by the holy prophets, and of the commandment of us the apostles of the Lord and Saviour:*

> 3 *Knowing this first, that there shall come in the last days scoffers, walking after their own lusts,*

> 4 *And saying, Where is the promise of his coming? for since the fathers fell asleep, all things continue as they were from the beginning of the creation.*

These last day scoffers were asking, "Where is the promise of His coming?" Now, remember this: God keeps His promises. Amen? If God promised that He would come, He's going to come. The scoffers were saying, "For since the fathers fell asleep, all things continue as they were from the beginning of creation."

> 5 *For this they willingly are ignorant of, that by the word of God the heavens were of old, and the earth standing out of the water and in the water:*

6 Whereby the world that then was, being overflowed with water, perished:

7 But the heavens and the earth, which are now, by the same word are kept in store, reserved unto fire against the day of judgment and perdition of ungodly men.

"But the heavens and the earth, which are now, by the same word, are kept in store." In other words, "All of this is still going on. The fact is that the heavens and earth, even now, are still being held together by the word of His promise, "Reserved unto fire against the day of judgment and perdition of ungodly men."

8 But, beloved, be not ignorant of this one thing, that one day is with the Lord as a thousand years, and a thousand years as one day.

9 The Lord is not slack concerning his promise, as some men count slackness; but is longsuffering to us-ward, not willing that any should perish, but that all should come to repentance.

"The Lord is not slack concerning His promise, as some men count slackness; but is longsuffering toward us." Some of the scoffers are saying, "When is He coming? Where is this going to happen?" They say, "I've heard that from the very beginning. As long as

I've been alive, I remember hearing those things." They're trying to say, "Because He hasn't shown up, it proves that God isn't real," whereas God is saying, "The reason I haven't shown up yet is because if I did, it wouldn't be good for you." Why? That is because there are scoffers. As long as there are scoffers, He's going to give them time to turn, to repent, and to come to Him.

The very thing that they're saying to prove that He doesn't exist is the one thing that proves Who He is and that He is Love. It proves that He is longsuffering and that He's putting up with it long enough to give every person who will turn the chance to turn. The rest of verse 9 tells us that the Lord is not willing that any should perish, but that all should come to repentance.

> *10 But the day of the Lord will come as a thief in the night; in the which the heavens shall pass away with a great noise, and the elements shall melt with fervent heat, the earth also and the works that are therein shall be burned up.*

Notice: "The day of the Lord will come as a thief in the night; in the which..." When it says, "*...in the which,*" it means *this is when it's going to happen.* Then it said, "...the heavens shall pass away with a great noise, and the elements shall melt with fervent heat, the earth also and the works that are therein shall be burned up."

>   *11 Seeing then that all these things shall be dissolved, what manner of persons ought ye to be in all holy conversation and godliness,*

"Seeing then that all these things shall be dissolved, what manner of persons ought you to be in all holy conversation [lifestyle] and godliness."   In other words, "By knowing what's going to take place, how should we live?   Knowing that, believing what God said is true, and knowing that God keeps His promises, how should we live on a day to day basis?"

>   *12 Looking for and hasting unto the coming of the day of God, wherein the heavens being on fire shall be dissolved, and the elements shall melt with fervent heat?*

>   *13 Nevertheless we, according to his promise, look for new heavens and a new earth, wherein dwelleth righteousness.*

>   *14 Wherefore, beloved, seeing that ye look for such things, be diligent that ye may be found of him in peace, without spot, and blameless.*

"Wherefore, beloved, seeing that you look for such things, be diligent." Notice that he didn't say be slothful, and he didn't say to just kick back and wait. He said, "Be diligent." He was telling them, "You believe what He has said, and you know that He has made this promise. Knowing that He keeps His promises, then you must be diligent that you may be found of Him in peace, without spot, and blameless."

Notice first of all that being "found of Him in peace without spot and blameless" is not an automatic thing. Apparently, there's something that you have to do to be "found of Him in peace, without spot, and blameless," because Peter was writing this after the Resurrection. If this had been automatic, then Peter would have just been wasting good parchment. Back then, parchment was expensive, and it was expensive to send letters.

If you were to write all of this on a parchment and then send it, you would count every word, literally. You would try to make things as short as possible, not to mention the fact that if he was not being accurate in this, then he was also confusing the people who would read it later on, people such as ourselves. If it had been automatic, he wouldn't even have had to mention it. Things that are automatically going to happen, you don't have to mention.

15 And account that the longsuffering of our Lord is salvation; even as our beloved brother Paul also according to the wisdom given unto him hath written unto you;

Notice here that Peter called him Brother Paul and not Apostle Paul. He called him a brother. People walk around saying, "I'm Apostle this; I'm Apostle that." Well, then just go and be an apostle and let people see that you're an apostle. Quit calling yourself an apostle and just be an apostle. An apple tree doesn't need a sign on it to say it's an apple tree. How do you know it's an apple tree? It has apples. Amen? It's easy to hang a tag on something, but if you have to tag it and put a name on it, it's probably because the person isn't doing what it takes for you to see the fruit in their life.

16 As also in all his epistles, speaking in them of these things; in which are some things hard to be understood, which they that are unlearned and unstable wrest, as they do also the other scriptures, unto their own destruction.

Even Peter was saying, "You know some of the things Paul says are hard to understand." When it said, "…which they that are unlearned and unstable wrest, as they do also the other Scriptures," it was showing that the people were taking the Scriptures and twisting them and making them say things that they were never meant to say. He went on to say that by doing so they were twisting them "unto their own destruction,"

> *17 Ye therefore, beloved, seeing ye know these things before, beware lest ye also, being led away with the error of the wicked, fall from your own stedfastness.*

I think sometimes that some of the doctrine that's out there is just there to test people's hearts. If you really want to know what's in a person, take away the rules. If you want to know how they really want to live, then take away all rules, take away all consequences of breaking the rules, and you'll find out what is in their heart. That's exactly what God did.

God said, "I can change your heart. You don't have to live by the law. I can change your heart, and if your heart is really changed by nature, you will keep the law without even thinking about it." Why? It is because you're not going to covet your neighbor's goods if your nature's changed. If your heart is right, you're not going to steal, and you're not going to bear false witness against people. Why? It is because it's part of your nature after being born again; you won't do those things. You don't have to be told, "Don't," because it's not in your nature to do them.

Nobody has to come up to me everyday and say, "Curry, don't drink, don't smoke, and don't go gambling." Nobody has to tell me that because it's not in my nature to do those things. I don't have to be on guard against them, because they are not even a temptation. They are not part of my nature.

18 But grow in grace, and in the knowledge of our Lord and Saviour Jesus Christ. To him be glory both now and for ever. Amen.

We are to grow "in grace, and in the knowledge of our Lord and Savior Jesus Christ."

Here's where the training part comes in. Any statement made by God, or by Jesus for God, that has the word *shall* or *will* in it is a promise. What do we know about the promises? "For all the promises of God *in* Him (Christ) are yes, and *in* Him (Christ) Amen (so be it), unto the glory of God by us."

In Christ, it is already considered by God yes and so be it, so it's not a matter of whether or not you are going to get an answer to prayer. It's a matter of you being *in* Christ and then finding out the promises of God, because once you find out the promise to you, it is automatically yes and so be it. It's not a matter of you trying to get God to do it, or you trying to twist His arm, or you doing something to live up to something to get Him to answer your prayer. You're *in* Him and because you're *in* Him, it's yes and so be it. Amen.

This message isn't about having a good sermon. This is about you being trained up. I know we're covering a lot of Scripture, but I want to give you the tools that you need. I want you to be able to live a victorious life in Christ Jesus. It is not just about going to church and hearing a sermon. I don't want you to go back home thinking that you've got your ticket punched for another week. I don't want you to think that if Jesus were to come between now and the next Sunday that you're good just because you were in church the Sunday before. That's not what this is about.

Hebrews 8:1-6,

> *1 Now of the things which we have spoken this is the sum: We have such an high priest, who is set on the right hand of the throne of the Majesty in the heavens;*

"Now of the things which we have spoken…" In other words, "Up to this point in the Book of Hebrews, this is the sum." If you believe that Paul wrote the Book of Hebrews, you could imagine him saying it like this: "Let me sum up what has been written in this book of Hebrews. We have a High Priest, and He is sitting on the right hand of the throne of God in heaven."

2 A minister of the sanctuary, and of the true tabernacle, which the Lord pitched, and not man.

3 For every high priest is ordained to offer gifts and sacrifices: wherefore it is of necessity that this man have somewhat also to offer.

"For every high priest is ordained," commissioned you might say, "to offer gifts and sacrifices: wherefore it is of necessity that this man have somewhat also to offer." If Jesus is the High Priest, He has to have something to offer, also.

4 For if he were on earth, he should not be a priest, seeing that there are priests that offer gifts according to the law:

5 Who serve unto the example and shadow of heavenly things, as Moses was admonished of God when he was about to make the tabernacle: for, See, saith he, that thou make all things according to the pattern shewed to thee in the mount.

6 But now hath he obtained a more excellent ministry, by how much also he is the mediator of a better covenant, which was established upon better promises.

"But now hath He [Jesus], obtained a more excellent ministry." Jesus' ministry is better than the ministry that the high priest had in the earthly tabernacle, the earthly temple. His is a better ministry. How? "By how much also He is the mediator of a better covenant..." What was this better covenant established upon? "It was established upon better promises." Think about that: "For all the promises of God *in* Him (Christ) are yes, and *in* Him (Christ) Amen (so be it), unto the glory of God by us." The promises we have are better promises than any promise they had under the Old Covenant.

If you go back and look at the promises under the Old Covenant, there were some pretty good promises there. Remember this: "For all the promises of God *in* Him are yes, and *in* Him so be it." Amen. Now, do you believe that? All the promises of God are *in* Him— that's where you are. Once you are *in* Him, the promises are there. It's not a matter of you getting them; they are already there! You stepped into them! It's like jumping into the ocean; you find yourself in the middle of water. That's the way it is when you get *in* Christ. You're in the middle of the promises of God. His promises are active; they are not things that are coming.

Deuteronomy 28:2,

> *2 And all these blessings shall come on thee, and overtake thee, if thou shalt hearken unto the voice of the LORD thy God.*

Even under the Old Covenant, they were promised that the blessings would overtake them, not that they would have to pursue them. However, in most churches around the world today, people are trying to teach others how to pursue the promises and how to get the blessings.

If you would just quit trying to outrun God and stop, the blessings would overtake you.

Years ago, John Osteen preached a message. I actually have the little booklet called, *A Place Called There*. Guess what? You will never be there, because as long as it's there, it's over there somewhere, and it's not here. Most Christians live their lives chasing a place called, *There*, rather than realizing that it's here. Amen.

Look at Hebrews 8:7-13,

> *7 For if that first covenant had been faultless, then should no place have been sought for the second.*

If the first covenant had been perfect, there wouldn't have been a need for any second covenant. This second covenant has better promises, and those promises are ours.

> *8 For finding fault with them, he saith, Behold, the days come, saith the Lord, when I will make a new covenant with the house of Israel and with the house of Judah:*

> *9 Not according to the covenant that I made with their fathers in the day when I took them by the hand to lead them out of the land of Egypt; because they continued not in my covenant, and I regarded them not, saith the Lord.*

> *10 For this is the covenant that I will make with the house of Israel after those days, saith the Lord; I will put my laws into their mind, and write them in their hearts: and I will be to them a God, and they shall be to me a people:*

This verse sounds like the one we read earlier in 2 Corinthians 6:16, where Paul said, "You are the temple of the living God; as God hath said, I will dwell *in* them, and walk *in* them; and I will be their God, and they shall be My people." In verse 17, He said, "Come out from among them and touch not the unclean thing, and I will receive you."

That time is the time of a New Covenant. That time is now. We're in the New Covenant; we're not in the Old Covenant. This is the time when He has written His laws upon our hearts.

> *11 And they shall not teach every man his neighbour, and every man his brother, saying, Know the Lord: for all shall know me, from the least to the greatest.*

In other words, "If you're in that Covenant, you're not going to have to be taught to know Him." Why? It is because to get into the Covenant, you have to know Him. Being in the Covenant is a union where God moves into you. People are always trying to get others to know God by saying, "We need to get into a deeper relationship with Him."

I can't teach you how to get into a deeper relationship with Him. That would be like someone asking, "How can you have a deeper relationship with a spouse?" Nobody can teach you how to do that. They can advise you about things that you should do that will help, but honestly, you just have to spend time with that person.

It comes down to you ceasing to be two and becoming one. That's how you get along with a spouse; you cease to be two. As long as you're two, you're going to have problems. Every problem you have is because you're not just like your spouse. I know that's deep, but do you get that? Every problem you have with your spouse is because you're not alike. If you were just like your spouse, you would get along perfectly.

This is true when you are talking about God, also. When you walk with God, you cease being two; you become one with Him. That means that you don't have your own thoughts anymore; you don't have your own will anymore. His thoughts become your thoughts, His will becomes your will, and you are one with Him. All of your struggles in Christianity go back to your un-renewed mind. You are fighting against Him, and You don't want to walk His path. That's your struggle.

For the most part, your struggle is not with the devil. You resist him, and I understand that, but the devil can't really do much to you that you don't let him do. Usually, your problem with the devil is that you side with him rather than with God. That's the big problem.

He says, "In this New Covenant, I'm going to write My laws on their hearts." That's how you know you're in the New Covenant—your nature is changed. There's a big difference between mentally assenting with Him and believing with Him. A lot of people mentally assent to the Bible, saying, "Every word is true. I believe every word of it." No, they don't. They agree with every word of it, but they don't believe every word of it.

You can agree with every word of it and still not have it working in your life. When you believe it is when it is working in your life. Until it's working in your life, you don't believe it; you just agree with it. Most people agree with it and think they believe it, and then they wonder why God doesn't hear their prayers. It's because they don't believe.

> *12 For I will be merciful to their unrighteousness, and their sins and their iniquities will I remember no more.*

In this New Covenant God doesn't remember your sins and iniquities, so if He doesn't remember them, you don't remember them! You have to choose to forget your past, and you may have to choose to forget your grandfather's past and everybody else's past. As we have taught in the Life Teams about generational curses, you have to realize that you don't have a generation if you are in Christ; you only go back to Jesus. That's it!

You're a new creation. What is born of the Spirit is spirit. God is a Spirit. Amen? You're born of Him, so go back to that generation. Don't go back to your earthly generation, and don't identify with them. The more you identify with them, the more problems you're going to have. That's the whole point of renewing your mind to the Word of God. You identify with your heavenly Father. You identify with your big Brother, and you start living His life.

> *13 In that he saith, A new covenant, he hath made the first old. Now that which decayeth and waxeth old is ready to vanish away.*

He was saying here that the Old Covenant was decaying and ready to vanish. If the Old Covenant is going away, that means there's going to be a new one. You can't have an old one if there's not a new one. He gave us a new one, so don't walk in the old—walk in the new.

Numbers 23:19-20,

> *19 God is not a man, that he should lie; neither the son of man, that he should repent: hath he said, and shall he not do it? or hath he spoken, and shall he not make it good?*

20 Behold, I have received commandment to bless: and he hath blessed; and I cannot reverse it.

When you get blessed of God, nobody can reverse it. You need to throw away those books that tell you why you're blocking God's blessings and why you're under a curse. If you believe that, all you're doing is allowing the devil to run through your life making you think, "Well, it must be a curse." If you're *in* Christ, Christ was made a curse for you. Why? It was so that you could be redeemed from the curse. You're not under a curse!

Think about this: it's like having a remote control. The television will be on and you will want to change channels. You will spend 15 minutes looking for the remote rather than getting up and walking three feet to the TV to push a button. Have you ever done that? That's what the devil does. He tells you that you've got a curse, and then he starts running around and messing up your life. You're running around trying to find out where the curse came from.

The whole point is that you didn't even have to worry about the devil. The curse isn't on you. He comes in, causes trouble, and tells you, "The problem's over there," and you spend time looking over there rather than looking at the real source. You need to stop and say, "Devil, get out! STOP your works in my life! You have no place here!" The devil will tell you, "Well, you know it's a curse." You say, "No! You're the curse! Get out!"

If being under a curse is your idea, that lets the devil keep running rampant through your life. You're not under a curse. How do we know that? That's because it says right here in Numbers, "Thou shalt not curse the people: for they *are* blessed." God has blessed His people; and it cannot be reversed (Numbers 23:20).

Numbers 22:9-12,

> 9 *And God came unto Balaam, and said, What men are these with thee?*

> 10 *And Balaam said unto God, Balak the son of Zippor, king of Moab, hath sent unto me, saying,*

> 11 *Behold, there is a people come out of Egypt, which covereth the face of the earth: come now, curse me them; peradventure I shall be able to overcome them, and drive them out.*

> 12 *And God said unto Balaam, Thou shalt not go with them; thou shalt not curse the people: for they are blessed.*

Even then, Balaam knew that God's people were blessed. He was told, "Curse these Israelites," and he said, "How can I curse those whom God has blessed?" Christians should awake to righteousness and realize the same thing and acknowledge, "How can we be cursed if we're blessed of God?"

Ephesians 1:3 says,

> *3 Blessed be the God and Father of our Lord Jesus Christ, who hath blessed us with all spiritual blessings in heavenly places in Christ:*

He did not say that you were cursed. You're blessed, and if God has blessed you, who can curse you? You ask, "Then what is all of this trouble in my life?" It's of the devil! Tell it to go! Tell it to stop. It may be sowing and reaping, and if it is, STOP IT! Stop doing it! Amen.

There are people who have to be taught a different mentality. Just the way they live creates problems in their lives. Then they sit around and ask, "Why doesn't God love me?" He does. "Then why is my life so messed up?" It's because you keep sowing the wrong seed. Turn around, do what's right, and live the way you're supposed to. Get out of this negative, poverty-driven mentality, and realize that you're blessed of God.

We went out to eat at a place and started talking to the girl who was a waitress there. She was upset because a well-known person who had been there didn't tip her. She let us know how bad this person was for not tipping even though this person had so much money. She just went on and on about it. She said, "He's got all of this money, but he's hanging on to it. The reason we don't have it is because God knows if we had it then we'd forget Him and go off into sin."

That is a wrong mentality. As long as you believe that, you will never prosper. God wants you to prosper, but you won't because you believe that prosperity is wrong. It shows the essence of your heart, because you believe that if you had money, you would forget God.

Proverbs 30:8-9,

> *8 Remove far from me vanity and lies: give me neither poverty nor riches; feed me with food convenient for me:*

> *9 Lest I be full, and deny thee, and say, Who is the LORD? or lest I be poor, and steal, and take the name of my God in vain.*

David said, "God, don't make me so poor that I would be tempted to steal, and don't make me so rich that I'd be tempted to forget You." God knows that, yet He still wants you to be blessed. He wants you to prosper.

Some people say, "God doesn't want me to prosper; just look at my life." God isn't controlling people's lives; they are controlling their own lives by not doing what God has said to do. They just need to be taught the basic principles that change a person's mentality.

God is not holding you down; you are holding yourself down. God wants to exalt you, but you keep holding yourself down.

It's one thing to be humble, and that's good, but don't think you're suffering so you can be humble. That's not the suffering that God wants you to suffer. He wants you to suffer persecution righteously, but He doesn't want you to suffer through sickness, disease, poverty, and hurt. He wants you to be able to bless. He wants you to be able to help people. That's what He wants for you.

John 14:12-15,

> *12 Verily, verily, I say unto you, He that believeth on me, the works that I do shall he do also; and greater works than these shall he do; because I go unto my Father.*

13 And whatsoever ye shall ask in my name, that will I do, that the Father may be glorified in the Son.

14 If ye shall ask any thing in my name, I will do it.

15 If ye love me, keep my commandments.

Remember: in Numbers 23:20, it said, "God has blessed, and I cannot reverse it." Why? "For all the promises of God *in* Him (Christ) are yes, and *in* Him, Amen (so be it)." I'm going to keep repeating this verse because you've got to get this message. "All the promises of God, *in* Christ, are yes," so whatever promise God has made, *in* Christ, the answer is yes. *In* Christ, the answer is *so be it* in your life. Not someday. No! So BE it! "BE" is now.

Any statement made by God or by Jesus for God that has the words *shall* or *will* in it is a promise. I know I've already said that. I'm not saying it accidentally. This needs to be drilled into you. You need to realize that when the Bible uses the words *shall* or *will,* it's as good as done. Jesus and the Father are just waiting for you to pick it up and agree.

Many people don't understand what it is like to talk about healing. People say, "If I don't feel healed, how can I say I am healed?" If that's where you are, that's okay. You are being prayed for, so you should be saying, "God is healing me." At least go that far. Maybe you don't want to say, "I am healed," but you can still say that you are being healed. It will take longer, but you'll still get it. At least agree. I'm just trying to help you. Amen.

The best thing is to agree with God 100 percent and say, "I'm healed by His stripes; it's done." If you can't go that far, and if you just can't see it, then at least agree with God and say, "He is healing me." Why? That's because you are in the process of being healed. You just say, "God has counted it done, but I'm in the process until I see it."

In Mark chapter 16, Jesus was speaking to His first disciples.

Mark 16:15-16,

> *15 And he said unto them, Go ye into all the world, and preach the gospel to every creature.*

> *16 He that believeth and is baptized shall be saved; but he that believeth not shall be damned.*

"He that believeth and is baptized…" What's the next word? The word is *shall*. "He that believeth and is baptized *shall* be saved." I want you to look at every one of these sentences as we read them, and notice the words, *shall* and *will*. "He that believeth and is baptized *shall* be saved." What does that mean? It means there is no way that you can believe, and be baptized, and not be saved. It goes on to say, "But he that believeth not *shall* be damned."

Both of the words used there are *shall*. That means that the word, *shall*, is the strongest word you can use in the English language. In other words, there is no way around it; this is what *will* happen. If someone does not believe, they *shall* be damned. It doesn't say that in the end it's all going to come together. It doesn't say that. That's universalism, and it's a heresy. God doesn't want anyone to perish. He wants them to come to repentance. That means that He wants them to turn around and be saved, not damned.

Mark 16:17,

> *17 And these signs shall follow them that believe; In my name shall they cast out devils; they shall speak with new tongues;*

"And these signs *shall* follow them that believe." Wait, are you sure it says, "S*hall*?" Most Christians act like it should say, "May, maybe, might, or it could happen." They might say, "Who knows? Maybe it will happen if God feels good today or if He's in a good mood." That's not what it says.

I want you to get this! I want you to get this down in you. You need to read and study these verses. You need to start telling God, the devil, and everybody around you the same thing. To the devil say, "Devil, listen in on our conversation." To God you say, "God, You said that I *shall* lay hands on the sick, and they *shall* recover. You said it! I didn't say it, and the devil didn't say it; YOU said it, and it's true." Someone might ask, "Why?" You can tell them, "That's because of the promises. 'For all the promises of God in him *are* yea, and in him so be it.'"

You say, "I'm in Christ and I believe, so I lay hands on the sick and they *shall* recover. End of story." They might come back and ask, "What if it doesn't happen? What if it's not God's will?" You say to them, "Don't even talk to me that way! How dare you say God is a liar to my face! How dare you say, 'What if it doesn't happen?' How can it not happen? God Himself has made a promise, and He's not a man that He should lie! God keeps His promises!"

At some point, you're just going to have to get bold enough, if need be, to be a little rude. You have to be able to stand up. Just take them right back to the Bible where it says, "These signs *shall* follow them that believe."

You have to get to that point where you will choose what God has said over what man says to you. If you do not get to that point, you will never move in the things of God. You won't see God work in your life. Why? That's because you're refusing to be a believer in His Word!

He said, "And these signs *shall*," absolutely, without a doubt, no *ifs, ands, or buts*, "follow them that believe; in My Name *shall* they cast out devils." Notice how believers cast out devils in His Name. It doesn't say that they might but that they *shall*.

It goes on to say, "They *shall* speak with new tongues." You might ask, "Do I have to speak in tongues to heal the sick?" No, but you *shall* speak with new tongues if you're a believer.

The people we talk about today are the ones who had the grit and the guts to stand against all of the people who said that they couldn't do it.

Smith Wigglesworth was one of those people. Nobody liked him. Nobody liked being around him, but they loved for him to pray for them. They loved for him to come in and do a healing service. They would stand back and watch miracles, but nobody was at his door. Nobody visited him. Why? He was rude.

As a matter of fact, almost all the men of God that I know of did exactly the same thing. It would get to a point, when people would visit, that they would hardly talk. Wigglesworth would talk for a few minutes, he would pray, and then he would read some Scripture. Then he would go back, pray some more, and then read more Scripture. Praying and reading Scripture is what you did when you were around him.

If somebody went to visit him, he would stay there with them for a little while, and then he would just stand up, close his Bible and say, "Well, it's about time that you leave." Imagine telling someone that.

John Wesley did the same thing. He would get up at a certain time every evening and he would say, "It's time for you to leave now because I have a previous appointment." He meant that he was going to go and pray. He didn't let people steal that away from him even if they thought of him as rude. He would go and spend time with God.

Most people are afraid of hurting people's feelings to the point where they end up not saying anything. If you're not saying anything then you're not hurting anybody's feelings, but you sure aren't helping anybody either.

Mark 16:18,

> *18 They shall take up serpents; and if they drink any deadly thing, it shall not hurt them; they shall lay hands on the sick, and they shall recover.*

He says in this verse: "They *shall* take up serpents; and if they drink any deadly thing, it *shall not* hurt them." Notice it said, "It *shall not* hurt them!" You need to just go through and drill these things in and say them with emphasis. It doesn't say that if you drink any deadly thing it might not hurt you; you might live through it. He said, "If they drink any deadly thing it *shall not* hurt them." Amen. "They *shall* lay hands on the sick, and they *shall* recover." Again, there are no *ifs, ands, or buts.* "They *shall* lay hands on the sick, and they *shall* recover!"

I remember talking with Dr. Sumrall about Smith Wigglesworth. He said that one time a man came up, Wigglesworth prayed for him, and then sent him on his way. The next night they were having another service and the same man came up for prayer. Wigglesworth started to pray for him, and then he said, "Wait. Didn't I pray for you last night?" The man said, "Well, yes." Wigglesworth said, "Well, go sit down." He said, "You're healed now and too dumb to know it." Why did he say that? It was because he had already prayed for him. He believed you only prayed once and that was it.

We can pray more than once. Jesus prayed twice, so we can pray twice. The main thing is that we pray and believe. Amen? You can pray a hundred times and if you don't believe, it doesn't matter. You have to decide to believe. Dr. Lake used to tell his congregation, "We have prayed. Now let's just take five minutes and believe God."

You can choose to believe God. If you can't choose to believe God at will, you didn't get saved when you thought you did. When you did get saved, you made a choice to submit your life to God. You can choose to believe Him. It should be an easy choice, because He has never lied. He keeps His promises, and you have to make that decision and say, "I am going to believe Him."

He is not slack in fulfilling His promises. We've been slack in believing Him. We've been slack in receiving Him and receiving His promises. You must receive His promise before you can see His promise. God keeps His promises. Amen.

Say it with me: "God keeps His promises." Say it again: "God Keeps His Promises." Now say it like you mean it: "GOD KEEPS HIS PROMISES!" Now just say this to yourself: "God keeps His promises to me!" "God Keeps His Promises to me!" "GOD KEEPS HIS PROMISES TO ME!" Amen.

I can't tell you the number of times I have gone to see people, laid hands on them, and then had to talk to them. Most of the time people will try to talk me out of their healing, and many times they will try to stay sick and fight me over their sickness and say, "I might not get healed because of this thing or that thing."

I tell them: "No, no, no, you don't understand. This has nothing to do with you. God made me a promise that whoever I lay hands on *shall* recover. He didn't name you. He didn't even put you in there. You're just here so God can fulfill His promise to me." Amen? Finally, I get them to a place where they say, "Oh, okay." Then I ask, "Will it be okay if I lay hands on you?" They say, "Yes, go ahead."

I lay hands on them and then they recover. Why? It is because of God's promise to me; it has nothing to do with them.

If they knew that God had promised to heal them that would be an entirely different thing. They could stand on that promise while I stand on God's promise to me, then we could agree, and it would be done. Amen?

Even if they don't know that they have a promise, I know I have a promise from God.

I know I have a promise from God to not only get healed if I get sick, but to stay well. I also know I have a promise from God to lay hands on the sick and they will get well, so it doesn't matter if they know the promise or not; I know the promise. That's what counts! It's between God and me, and God keeps His promises! Amen.

Again, any statement made by God or made by Jesus for Him that has the word *shall* or *will* in it is a promise. It's something you can stand on. In Christ it's already considered, by God, as yes and so be it. Watch for the *shall's* and *will's*.

Mark 11:22-23,

> 22 *And Jesus answering saith unto them, Have faith in God.*

"Have faith in God." I've known people who tried to turn that around and say, "Have the faith of God." Bottom line, it comes down to you. You have to have faith in God, not in your faith. You have to have faith in God, Himself, and in His Word.

23 For verily I say unto you, That whosoever shall say unto this mountain, Be thou removed, and be thou cast into the sea; and shall not doubt in his heart, but shall believe that those things which he saith shall come to pass; he shall have whatsoever he saith.

Jesus was saying, "For verily I say unto you, That whosoever *shall* say," not think, but say, "unto this mountain, Be thou removed, and be thou cast into the sea; and shall not doubt in his heart, but *shall* believe that those things which he saith *shall*," there's that word *shall* which means that it is a promise, "come to pass."

Do you realize that your faith is activated at the point of *shall?* Why? It's because that's a promise and that's what you activate your faith on, the fact that it *shall* be done. You say, "I have it now, and it *shall* be done. I receive it now as done, and it *shall* be." That's what Jesus was saying here—but first you have to receive it as done, now. In other words, "Yes, it's done, and I *shall* have it. You've already made the call, you've ordered the thing. You've given your card number and they have said, "Okay, we *will* put it in the mail on Monday." You say, "Guess what I just bought? I just bought this, and on Monday, I *shall* have it."

We ordered some equipment last week. We ordered it, we paid for, it's ours, and it's en route to us even now. It's supposed to be here tomorrow. That means we have bought it, and we *shall* have it. We're already talking about how to use it and watching training videos on YouTube. I'm saying, "This is a neat thing. It's going to be fun." It's ours. It's got our name on it. It's already left the manufacturer, so it's en route.

Daniel 10:11-13,

> *11 And he said unto me, O Daniel, a man greatly beloved, understand the words that I speak unto thee, and stand upright: for unto thee am I now sent. And when he had spoken this word unto me, I stood trembling.*

> *12 Then said he unto me, Fear not, Daniel: for from the first day that thou didst set thine heart to understand, and to chasten thyself before thy God, thy words were heard, and I am come for thy words.*

> *13 But the prince of the kingdom of Persia withstood me one and twenty days: but, lo, Michael, one of the chief princes, came to help me; and I remained there with the kings of Persia.*

Think back to when Daniel prayed for 21 days. The angel showed up and said, "Daniel, God heard your prayers, and I was sent. Your prayer was answered." When was it answered? It was answered the day that Daniel prayed. The angel was saying, "It's just taken me this long to get here." Was it done as far as God was concerned? Yes, but it still had to be brought through into the now.

You have to realize: "They *shall* lay hands on the sick, and they *shall* recover." As far as God's concerned that's a promise and it's done. When I lay hands on the sick, it's ratified in heaven, and healing is on its way.

When you say, "I got my healing," someone else might say, "Well, you don't look healed." You answer: "It doesn't matter what I look like; what counts is that I got the answer. What counts is that it's as good as done." They ask, "Why?" That's when you say, "Because I believe it, I *shall* have it." They say, "Well, I don't believe that." You say, "Well, it's good that it's not you that's sick then. Hide and watch me. I'll get well." They will question you and ask, "Why?" You tell them: "I know, because I *shall* have it." I'm just telling you what basic faith is. This is how it works. Let's go back to Mark 11.

Mark 11:23,

> *23 For verily I say unto you, That whosoever shall say unto this mountain, Be thou removed, and be thou cast into the sea; and shall not doubt in his heart, but shall believe that those things which he saith shall come to pass; he shall have whatsoever he saith.*

"Be thou removed, and be thou cast into the sea; and *shall* not doubt in his heart, but *shall* believe that those things which he saith *shall* come to pass." Notice it doesn't say, "*Shall not* doubt in his head." Do you realize that you can have doubts in your head and still not be doubting in your heart? People will tell you why it won't work or how it's not going to happen. Even if you take that thought by saying and agreeing with them, your heart will still believe, and no matter what your head is saying, you will still decide to believe God.

"That whosoever *shall* say unto this mountain, Be thou removed, and be thou cast into the sea; and *shall* not doubt in his heart, But *shall* believe that those things which he saith *shall* come to pass; he *shall* have whatsoever he saith." Look at this: five times it says *shall* in this verse. *Shall* is the strongest word in the English language. He used it five times in one verse, so how sure do you think that promise is? That should tell you that you have to get to believing and saying, "I've got to get busy saying some things, because I believe that what I say *will* come to pass." Amen?

Mark 11:24,

> *24 Therefore I say unto you, What things soever ye desire, when ye pray, believe that ye receive them, and ye shall have them.*

Jesus said, "Therefore I say unto you…" Why? That's because whatever you desire or pray for *will* come to pass. Notice that it was Jesus, not just anybody, Who said: "What things soever you desire." Look how big that is. "What things soever you desire," means whatever it is. Think about that. That's just a blank check from God. You will get whatever it is that you desire, and it will be when you pray, not later, not when you see it, but when you pray. It says, "Believe that you receive them, and you *shall* have them." God is not telling you to lie; He's telling you how to operate in faith.

Anybody can believe when they see; that's what the world does. You're not of the world. You've got to believe before you see—that's what makes you different from the world.

"When you pray, believe that you receive them, and you *shall* have them." Notice that first you believe that you've received them. You know that you will have them, but you recognize that you're not going to have them right then. The promise is: "And you *shall* have them."

John 14:12-14,

> *12 Verily, verily, I say unto you, He that believeth on me, the works that I do shall he do also; and greater works than these shall he do; because I go unto my Father.*

"Verily, verily, I say unto you," this was Jesus speaking, "He that believeth on me, the works that I do *shall* he do also; and greater works than these *shall* he do." Why? He said, "Because I go to My Father."

> *13 And whatsoever ye shall ask in my name, that will I do, that the Father may be glorified in the Son.*

We have a problem with that because it's so open-ended, but if Jesus had made every promise specific, the Bible would be so thick that we wouldn't even be able to carry it around. True great faith is being able to take a general promise and apply it to a specific situation, and the more general the promise that you can apply to a specific situation, the greater faith you're operating in. If you want to know how to grow in faith, start using more general promises rather than specific promises.

In the group I was in before, we had to have a verse for everything. They would ask, "What verse are you standing on?" It had to be specific and cover that one thing. It was bondage.

The greatest faith is taking a general promise and applying it. "They *shall* lay hands on the sick, and they *shall* recover." That's as general as you can get, and I stand on that. I apply that general promise to individual people who stand in front of me, and because of that, they recover. Amen.

"That *will* I do." It is not, "I might do it." It's not, "Maybe." No, it says, "That *will* I do." Why? He tells you that He's going to do whatever you ask. Here's why He does it: "That the Father may be glorified in the Son." It's not so He can do something just for you.

14 If ye shall ask any thing in my name, I will do it.

Notice: "If you *shall* ask anything in My name, I *will* do it." Do you realize He says this in three verses over, and over, and over? He says, "Anything you ask

I *will* do." The Father is going to be glorified in the Son. Over and over again He says it.

If you get hold of this message, I will tell you right now that your days of unanswered prayers are over.

I do not know of one prayer that I've ever prayed that did not come to pass. People say, "Haven't you prayed for people and they died?" I don't pray for people. If you've gone through the DHT (Divine Healing Technician Training), you know that we don't pray for people. We don't pray for your healing. We command healing; we command your body to be healed. We command, and we speak the end result, but we're not praying.

I'm not going to talk to God about your healing. Why? The number one reason is because of the promise: "Lay hands on the sick, and they *shall* recover." This takes us back to what we read before.

2 Corinthians 1: 20,

> *20 For all the promises of God in him are yea, and in him Amen, unto the glory of God by us.*

"For all the promises of God in Christ *are* yes, and in Christ so be it." I don't have to ask Him about that.

Like I said, I don't know of one prayer that I've ever prayed that did not come to pass. Some say that they have had unanswered prayer. God never intended for you to have unanswered prayers, not one! He wants every prayer answered. Jesus wants to answer them so that the Father will be glorified in the Son.

1 John 5:14-15,

> *14 And this is the confidence that we have in him, that, if we ask any thing according to his will, he heareth us:*

> *15 And if we know that he hear us, whatsoever we ask, we know that we have the petitions that we desired of him.*

In other words, "If we ask any thing according to His will, he hears us, and if we know that God hears us when we pray, we know we have what we ask." The basic key is making sure that what you pray is heard by God. Anything that you get God to hear gets done.

John 14:15-21,

> *15 If ye love me, keep my commandments.*

> *16 And I will pray the Father, and he shall give you another Comforter, that he may abide with you for ever;*

Notice, "I *will* pray and He *shall* give you another Comforter." Do you hear that? *Will* and *shall* are in the same verse. Jesus said, "I *will* pray the Father, and He *shall* give you another Comforter." What kind of Comforter would He send? He said that He would send One Who will "abide with you forever." That means you're never alone. He doesn't come and go.

> *17 Even the Spirit of truth; whom the world cannot receive, because it seeth him not, neither knoweth him: but ye know him; for he dwelleth with you, and shall be in you.*

Notice: the world can't receive Him because it doesn't see Him. Don't be like the world and think that just because you don't see Him, you don't have Him. "Neither knows Him: but you know Him; for He dwells with you, and *shall*," there's that word again, "be *in* you." Do you hear that promise? His Spirit *shall* be *in* you. If you're *in* Him, and His Spirit is *in* you. Amen.

> *18 I will not leave you comfortless: I will come to you.*

> *19 Yet a little while, and the world seeth me no more; but ye see me: because I live, ye shall live also.*

Do you hear these promises? All of these are yours. He said that these were for you to walk in and live in.

> *20 At that day ye shall know that I am in my Father, and ye in me, and I in you.*

Jesus said, "You *in* me, and I *in* you." What does that mean? That means that you're hidden; you're *in* Him. You're hidden and the devil can't find you. Your sins and iniquities are gone. Do you realize that you stand before God clean, pure, and holy in Christ Jesus? The devil can't put anything on you. God won't remember it, so don't bring it up. If you remember it, it's because the devil is telling you to. Just choose not to remember it.

When He said, "I," He was talking about His Spirit. "Then in that day you'll know that you're *in* Me and I am *in* you." When He said, "I'm *in* you," He meant that He, the Comforter, He, the power of God Himself, is *in* you to accomplish His will on this earth.

We talk about you being the temple of the Living God and that His Spirit lives *in* you. Why is He *in* you? It is so that His will can be done on this earth and so that greater works can be done through you: healings, deliverances, and salvation. You can set the captives free from bondage, addictions, habits, and of all these bad things.

God wants you to live free. He wants you to be healthy. He wants you to be strong. He wants you to live with prosperity. He wants you to live blessed so you can be a blessing. That's the key. We're not here to be blessed; we're blessed because we're *in* Him. We are blessed to be a blessing.

> *21 He that hath my commandments, and keepeth them, he it is that loveth me: and he that loveth me shall be loved of my Father, and I will love him, and will manifest myself to him.*

Do you want Jesus to manifest Himself? It's simple; keep His commandments.

Mark 12:30-31,

> *30 And thou shalt love the Lord thy God with all thy heart, and with all thy soul, and with all thy mind, and with all thy strength: this is the first commandment.*

> *31 And the second is like, namely this, Thou shalt love thy neighbour as thyself. There is none other commandment greater than these.*

What are His commandments? "Love the Lord thy God with all your heart, soul, mind, and strength, and your neighbor as yourself." You are to do unto others as you would have them do unto you. If you live that way, He will manifest Himself to you. It's the easiest thing in the world to get. God keeps His promises.

In Hebrews 6:12-15,

> *12 That ye be not slothful, but followers of them who through faith and patience inherit the promises.*

The word, *patience*, there means *consistency*. "Follow the faith of those who through faith and patience (consistency) inherit the promises." *Follow the Faith of the Faithful* CD is available (recorded Dec. 29, 2013). This would be a good one for you to listen to.

> *13 For when God made promise to Abraham, because he could swear by no greater, he sware by himself,*

Notice what God did: He made a promise to Abraham.

> *14 Saying, Surely blessing I will bless thee, and multiplying I will multiply thee.*

> *15 And so, after he had patiently endured, he obtained the promise*

Every prophecy in the Bible is a promise that God's going to do something, and God keeps His promises.

Joel 2:28,

> *28 And it shall come to pass afterward, that I will pour out my spirit upon all flesh; and your sons and your daughters shall prophesy, your old men shall dream dreams, your young men shall see visions:*

He said, "I will pour out My Spirit on all flesh." Although we call it a prophecy, that was a promise, and He kept His word. There's not one person who cannot have and experience the Spirit of God dwelling within them. If anyone doesn't, it's because of their own choice not to do what He said to do which is simply to invite Him in.

Hebrews 6:16-18,

> *16 For men verily swear by the greater: and an oath for confirmation is to them an end of all strife.*

In other words, once you swear an oath, that's it. There's no more arguing about it; it's done.

> *17 Wherein God, willing more abundantly to shew unto the heirs of promise the immutability of his counsel, confirmed it by an oath:*

"Wherein God, willing more abundantly to show unto the heirs," that's you, "of promise." In other words, "He's going to show to you (you who are going to be the heirs) what God has guaranteed that He will do. He will show it with the immutability of His counsel, confirmed by an oath."

> *18 That by two immutable things, in which it was impossible for God to lie, we might have a strong consolation, who have fled for refuge to lay hold upon the hope set before us:*

It is impossible for God to lie.

In Deuteronomy 28, we read about promises of God. Remember: Jesus was made a curse for us so that we might inherit the blessings of God, the promises of God.

Deuteronomy 28:1- 14,

> *1 And it shall come to pass, if thou shalt hearken diligently unto the voice of the LORD thy God, to observe and to do all his commandments which I command thee this day, that the LORD thy God will set thee on high above all nations of the earth:*

"And it *shall* come to pass, if you *shall* hearken diligently to the voice of the Lord thy God..." If you're born again, you've done that; you've listened to His voice. You have come to His Son; you are *in* Christ. "...to observe and to do all His commandments which I command you this day, that the Lord thy God *will* set thee on high above all nations of the earth." Now, count the number of times where you see the words *will* and *shall*.

> *2 And all these blessings shall come on thee, and overtake thee, if thou shalt hearken unto the voice of the LORD thy God.*

> *3 Blessed shalt thou be in the city, and blessed shalt thou be in the field.*

He said that you're going to be blessed in the city and blessed in the field. Guess what that means? You're blessed everywhere! There's no where you can go that you're not blessed.

Someone might say, "Well, you don't understand; this is a hard place." It was a hard place for somebody in the world and for somebody not under the blessings of God, but for a person under the blessings of God, every place is an easy place. Why? That's because you're not laboring. You have entered into His rest, and you're just there seeing that His work is done. You are God's steward, doing His work.

Nothing is impossible with God. In John 14:10, Jesus said, "The Father that dwelleth in me, He doeth the works." If you were doing them, then it might be hard for you, but if it's God, *in* you, doing them, then it's easy; it's not a hard place. It would be hard for a human. It might even be impossible for a human, but with God, all things are possible.

> *4 Blessed shall be the fruit of thy body, and the fruit of thy ground, and the fruit of thy cattle, the increase of thy kine, and the flocks of thy sheep.*

"Blessed shall be the fruit of your body." Do you hear that? You need to call the fruit of your body blessed. I don't care if you are 50 or 60 years old and you've got 30 year old kids, you need to call the fruit of your body blessed. My children are blessed. Amen? My grandchildren are blessed. Why? That's because they came from me, and they're not going to see the sins of their father. They're going to see that their father obeys the Word of God, (this is out of Ezekiel 18), and they're going to choose to go that way, and because of that, they will be blessed, and they will live in righteousness. Amen.

"Blessed you'll be in the city, and blessed in the field, blessed will be the fruit of your body, the fruit of your ground, and the fruit of your cattle, the increase of thy kine, and the flocks of your sheep." In other words, anything you own *shall* be blessed.

5 Blessed shall be thy basket and thy store.

The place where you work *shall* be blessed because you work there, even if you don't own it. Your employer ought to recognize that. That's what happened with Joseph. They recognized that everything he did was blessed. They said, "We need to promote him, because everything under him is blessed, and we want everything above him to be blessed, also. Let's elevate him; let's promote him." That's what should be going on with you on your job. Wherever you're working, it should be blessed. Everything you have authority over should be blessed and they should recognize that and say, "We're going to promote you, because everything you touch turns to gold." They will promote you and say, "Yes, this is because of your faith in God." You have got to change your mentality and start thinking Kingdom.

6 Blessed shalt thou be when thou comest in, and blessed shalt thou be when thou goest out.

7 The LORD shall cause thine enemies that rise up against thee to be smitten before thy face: they shall come out against thee one way, and flee before thee seven ways.

> *8 The LORD shall command the blessing upon thee in thy storehouses, and in all that thou settest thine hand unto; and he shall bless thee in the land which the LORD thy God giveth thee.*

It uses that word, *shall,* again. "The Lord *shall* command the blessing upon you in your storehouses, and He *shall* bless you in the land which the LORD your God gives you." That could be your pantry of food, it could be your bank account, it could be your savings account, or it could be your 401K. Whatever your storehouse is, you ought to be saying, "That's blessed."

You might say, "Well, we're going to take that." No, we aren't finished yet. What I am giving you is going to be pressed down, shaken together, and running over (Luke 6:38). You might figure on taking this now, but I'm going to be giving you more. When we get finished here, we are going to have more than what we started with. You're going to scratch your heads and wonder, "How?" That's because I'm depending on God.

"The LORD *shall* command the blessing in all that you set your hand to." Do you hear that? He said, "The LORD *shall*..." That means that He *will* command the blessing to everything that you put your hand to. Put your hand to people—He will command the blessing upon them. Put your hand to your job. Put your hand to your house or to your car.

If you don't think your car is going to make it, put your hand to it. Bless it in Jesus' name, and God will say, "That thing's gone. I'll give you a new one." There are some times when you say, "God, I want You to bless this, but I had much rather that You bless me with a better one." You don't have to keep driving the same car that you have to keep working on.

"The LORD *shall* command the blessing upon thee and in all that you set your hand to, and He *shall* bless you in the land which your God has given you."

> 9 *The LORD shall establish thee an holy people unto himself, as he hath sworn unto thee, if thou shalt keep the commandments of the LORD thy God, and walk in his ways.*

> 10 *And all people of the earth shall see that thou art called by the name of the LORD; and they shall be afraid of thee.*

In the Book of Acts, great fear came upon all people of the earth. Why? It was because of the Church and what God was doing in the Church. It was time for the world to take notice. It is the same today. You don't touch the Church. Why? That's because God backs us up. God is behind us. Don't touch the Church. Amen? "All people of the earth shall know the Name of the LORD, and they *shall* be afraid."

> *11 And the LORD shall make thee plenteous in goods, in the fruit of thy body, and in the fruit of thy cattle, and in the fruit of thy ground, in the land which the LORD sware unto thy fathers to give thee.*
>
> *12 The LORD shall open unto thee his good treasure, the heaven to give the rain unto thy land in his season, and to bless all the work of thine hand: and thou shalt lend unto many nations, and thou shalt not borrow.*

"You *shall* lend to many nations, and you *shall* not borrow." Some of you need to be going after that and saying, "I lend. I don't have to borrow." Almost every car we've bought we've paid cash for. I do not go into debt. I don't believe in debt. I don't ever intend to go into debt. We believe God, and we see it met; we don't go into debt. Why? That's because He said that we don't have to borrow; we will lend. That means that I have enough extra, above what I need, to lend.

You need to say, "God, You said this, and You keep Your promises. I thank You for them, and God, I'm keeping Your commandments. I'm *in* Christ, I love You, I love my fellowman, and I'm blessing people. I am giving freely. I'm doing all of these things, so God, I just expect to be able to bless, and to give, and not have to borrow."

I will tell you this: I don't lend money; I give money. If you get money from me, it is because I give it to you. I don't expect it back. Why? God doesn't expect it back from me. I treat you the way I want to be treated. God gives it to me—I give it to you; it's that simple. I don't lend money because lending tends to make people feel weird. If you lend it and they think they're supposed to pay it back, then they start avoiding you if they can't pay it back.

I had rather give you the money and keep your friendship rather than to have you borrow money and have that weird thing going on. I want to treat you the way God treats me.

13 And the LORD shall make thee the head, and not the tail; and thou shalt be above only, and thou shalt not be beneath; if that thou hearken unto the commandments of the LORD thy God, which I command thee this day, to observe and to do them:

14 And thou shalt not go aside from any of the words which I command thee this day, to the right hand, or to the left, to go after other gods to serve them.

Luke 10:19,

19 Behold, I give unto you power to tread on serpents and scorpions, and over all the power of the enemy: and nothing shall by any means hurt you.

This is a promise of God: "Behold," look or take notice, "I give," not I loan, "I give unto you power," authority or permission, "to tread on serpents and scorpions, and over all the power," ability, "of the enemy: and NOTHING shall by any means hurt you." That's a promise that you need to get hold of. God keeps His promises.

I lay hands on people who have all kinds of diseases, and the germs should be able to jump back on me. I have to believe this verse when it says that nothing shall by any means hurt me. I don't need health insurance; I've got Psalms 91, and I've got Luke 10:19. I've got a premium and a secondary. I've never had health insurance. The only life insurance I ever had was when I was in the military and when I worked for the State of Texas. I don't have any of that now. God is my only safety net. Nobody is going to tell me to have a different one. I will trust God. It is that simple.

What were you promised in verse 19? "Nothing shall by any means hurt you."

Acts 1:8,

> 8 *But ye shall receive power, after that the Holy Ghost is come upon you: and ye shall be witnesses unto me both in Jerusalem, and in all Judaea, and in Samaria, and unto the uttermost part of the earth.*

"But you *shall*," not maybe, "*shall* receive power," miraculous ability, "after that the Holy Ghost is come upon you: and you *shall* be witnesses unto Me both in Jerusalem, and in all Judea, and in Samaria, and unto the uttermost part of the earth." It says, "You *shall,*" not maybe, but you *shall.*

Matthew 17:19- 20,

> 19 *Then came the disciples to Jesus apart, and said, Why could not we cast him out?*

20 And Jesus said unto them, Because of your unbelief: for verily I say unto you, If ye have faith as a grain of mustard seed, ye shall say unto this mountain, Remove hence to yonder place; and it shall remove; and nothing shall be impossible unto you.

"And Jesus said unto them, Because of your unbelief: for verily I say unto you, If you have faith as a grain of mustard seed, you shall *say...*" Do you hear that? If you have faith you shall *say…*"

People say, "Well, I have faith, but I just keep it quiet. It's a personal thing." No! If you have faith you shall *say.* If you shall not say, you shall not have faith. Faith speaks.

2 Corinthians 4:13,

13 We having the same spirit of faith, according as it is written, I believed, and therefore have I spoken; we also believe, and therefore speak;

Paul said, "I believed, and therefore have I *spoken*; we also believe, and therefore *speak.*" In other words, "Because we have believed, we *speak.*" If you believe something, you *speak.*

"You shall *say* unto this mountain, Remove hence to yonder place." Then it says, "It *shall* remove; and nothing *shall* be impossible to you." Do you hear that? "Nothing *shall* be impossible to you."

What would you do if you knew you couldn't fail? What would you launch out into if you knew that no matter what you put your hand to, it would prosper? It wouldn't matter what you did, it would work.

Nothing can hurt you, and nothing is impossible. You could say, "There is no way that I could do this with what I have." You need to decide what you need to do with what you have and do it. Why? That's because the problem might seem impossible to you, but it's not impossible with Him. Whenever that impossible thing happens, then you will know that God did it. Guess who will get the glory? God will get the glory. You need to start doing the impossible. You need to find the impossible, go to your limits, find what you can't do, and then do it. Amen.

You need to go beyond you. Stop playing it safe. People say, "We've got this buffer zone." The buffer zone is the *No Faith Zone*. You have to get into faith. Step out. Get into the deep end, as they would say.

Luke 1:37,

> *37 For with God nothing shall be impossible.*

Luke 6:38,

> *38 Give, and it shall be given unto you; good measure, pressed down, and shaken together, and running over, shall men give into your bosom. For with the same measure that ye mete withal it shall be measured to you again.*

It says, "Give, and it *shall* be given unto you." Then it says, "For with the same measure that you mete withal it *shall* be measured to you again."

Say it with me: "God keeps His promises!" Say it again. "God Keeps His Promises!" Say it like you mean it. "GOD KEEPS HIS PROMISES!" Say, "He keeps His promises to me." Amen.

Chapter 2

Have Faith in God

Have Faith in God, because God keeps His promises.

Mark 11:11,

> *11 And Jesus entered into Jerusalem, and into the temple: and when he had looked round about upon all things, and now the eventide was come, he went out unto Bethany with the twelve.*

Jesus went into Jerusalem, looked around, came back out and went into Bethany.

> *12 And on the morrow, when they were come from Bethany, he was hungry:*

> *13 And seeing a fig tree afar off having leaves, he came, if haply he might find any thing thereon: and when he came to it, he found nothing but leaves; for the time of figs was not yet.*

> *14 And Jesus answered and said unto it, No man eat fruit of thee hereafter for ever. And his disciples heard it.*

Notice: "Jesus answered and said…" He answered the fig tree, even though the fig tree didn't say anything. The fact was that it did not produce the fruit that it should have. You say, "Well, maybe it wasn't the time for figs." That's true, but trees were created to feed man, and it did not feed man, the Son of Man in this case. Jesus answered and spoke unto it.

Think about this: Jesus, King of kings, Lord of lords, and God in the flesh talked to a tree. He was standing there looking at a tree and talking to the tree. Maybe you won't feel so bad about talking to your car, or your washing machine, or your dryer. The difference might be in what you are saying to it and how you say it. Be careful what you say; you might actually get what you ask for from then on. Don't call it stupid. Don't talk about how it never works. If you are going to say, "You stupid thing, you just never work right," you might as well just throw it out and get another one because you have already cursed that one.

"Jesus answered and said unto it, 'No man eat fruit of thee hereafter forever.'" Was that a request or a command? It says, "And his disciples heard it." What does that mean? It means that He didn't whisper. It means that He wasn't ashamed to talk out loud to it. He just spoke to it, like He would speak to a person.

He commanded it not to produce fruit nor allow any person to eat from it from then on.

> *15 And they come to Jerusalem: and Jesus went into the temple, and began to cast out them that sold and bought in the temple, and overthrew the tables of the moneychangers, and the seats of them that sold doves;*

The doves were used for sacrifices.

> *16 And would not suffer that any man should carry any vessel through the temple.*

> *17 And he taught, saying unto them, Is it not written, My house shall be called of all nations the house of prayer? but ye have made it a den of thieves.*

> *18 And the scribes and chief priests heard it, and sought how they might destroy him: for they feared him, because all the people was astonished at his doctrine.*

People usually try to destroy what they are afraid of, and here's why they were afraid: "All the people were astonished at his doctrine." They knew that they were losing their positions.

It tells what He did chronologically. It says that He went into the city, came back out, cursed the fig tree, went back into the city the next day, and came back out. A good twenty-four hours had passed.

> *19 And when even was come, he went out of the city.*

> *20 And in the morning, as they passed by, they saw the fig tree dried up from the roots.*

On the morning of the next day, it says, "They saw the fig tree dried up from the roots." I am going to be emphasizing points based on exactly what it says. It said that on the day before, Jesus spoke to the fig tree and the disciples heard it.

First, they heard, and then 24 hours or so later, they saw. They didn't see first and then hear. They heard Him say it, and then they saw it, twenty-fours later. When He first said it, they were standing there, and they heard it. Then, He walked off and nothing changed. They didn't see any difference. The tree was still there, and it still looked the same. It didn't fall over. They probably walked by and said, "Well, that was weird. He was just talking to a fig tree and telling it to do things. He told it not to have fruit. It already doesn't have fruit, so I don't see any difference."

Notice where it was dried up from: the drying up of the fig tree started at the roots, so basically, He cut the life off at the roots with His words. It took at least 24 hours for all of the life to drain out of the limbs. If you cut down a tree in your front yard, it will still look like a tree for a couple of days until all the life drains out of it, and then it will start looking like a dead tree.

How many of you know that I am not talking about a tree? I am talking about cancer. I am talking about tumors. I am talking about different situations that you go through in your life. You speak to it—you say what it has to do—and then you will see. If you only say what you see, you will never have anything other than what you see. You speak to the thing.

Most people will speak to something and then they will turn around and say, "I don't see any difference. Didn't you just lay hands on me? Didn't you just command that thing to go? Why is it still there?" Sometimes it takes a little time for the life that is already in it to drain out of it before it will fall away. At other times, when a working of miracles is taking place, it can dissolve instantly.

Today we read about a woman who was working in another room when she was healed. She was not even thinking about a miracle when it happened. That was a gift of the Holy Spirit working. It was an instantaneous miracle.

In verse 14, they heard Jesus say it, and in verse 20, they saw it. First, you *say*, and then you see it. For anyone to see it, someone has to *say* it. Until someone *says* it, nobody is going to see it. You have to decide if you are going to be the person who is willing to step out and *say* it before anybody can see it. When you *say* it before anybody can see it, and later they see it, they are going to refer back to you and say, "That is just like he said it would be. Yesterday or the day before he said that, and now look at it." You will start to develop a reputation as a person of faith.

> *21 And Peter calling to remembrance saith unto him, Master, behold, the fig tree which thou cursedst is withered away.*

Jesus said, "No man eat fruit of you hereafter forever," and yet, Peter said that was a curse. All Jesus said of the tree was: "Let no man eat of it." Trees were created for man; you can read that in Genesis. Jesus was saying that the tree could not fulfill its divine reason for its existence. Let's define curse. *Curse* means *to say something negative that contradicts something's divine reason for its existence.*

When you tell someone that they will never amount to anything, you curse them. If you curse them enough, it will get into them. They will start believing it. If you keep chipping away, before long their image of themselves will be exactly what you have been saying. They will give up even trying to do anything. Then if you say, "See, I told you," it becomes a self-fulfilling prophecy, when it was your mouth that caused their attitude.

I am not saying that everybody is susceptible. Everybody is responsible for their own selves, but when that's all a person hears, it starts to get to them. That's why they need to have the guts and the grit sometimes to get away from people who only talk doubt and unbelief, and tell them what they can't do. They need to start *saying* what God has said they can do.

Don't curse. I had rather hear somebody cuss than curse, and I don't like cussing. I have never been a cusser, even when I was in the military. It was normal to hear it there, but it just didn't feel right, especially around mixed company. I just didn't get it. People will say anything, and many times it is in mixed company.

Look at verse 22. This proves that Jesus was not operating out of a gift of the working of miracles or any other gift, per se. Peter had just said, "Master, behold (look), the fig tree which you cursed is withered away."

> *22 And Jesus answering saith unto them, Have faith in God.*

Jesus answered him by saying, "Have faith in God." He didn't say, "If you get the Spirit of God, you can have a gift operating, too." He didn't say that. He told Peter, "Have faith in God." What does that mean? It means that Jesus had faith in God when He spoke.

> *23 For verily I say unto you, That whosoever shall say unto this mountain, Be thou removed, and be thou cast into the sea; and shall not doubt in his heart, but shall believe that those things which he saith shall come to pass; he shall have whatsoever he saith.*

In the first of the series, we emphasized *shall* and *will?* Those are promises, and God keeps His promises. "Whosoever *shall* say (not think about, not wish, but say) unto this mountain, Be thou removed," which is a command, "and be thou cast into the sea," another command, "and *shall not* doubt in his heart, but *shall* believe..." Believe what? "That those things which he saith *shall* come to pass; he *shall* have whatsoever he saith."

The first part here is not talking about prayer. Prayer doesn't come until the next verse. He was talking about your normal state of speaking. He was talking about how you normally speak on a daily basis. In your normal life, you have to *say* what you want to come to pass and believe that what you *say* will come to pass. Jesus Himself was *saying* this, and that showed His faith in God. You have to have faith in God that He will cause your words to come to pass.

There was a prophet in the Old Testament and it was actually said about him that God did not let one of his words fall to the ground. He didn't just pick somebody and say, "Your words aren't going to fall to the ground." It wasn't that at all. It was that God's Spirit was with that person and that person said the things that God wanted said. It is easy for God to back you up when you say what He would say if He were here.

When I go to minister to somebody, I am not trying to think up words just so I can come up with my own words. All I am doing is what Jesus would do if He were here. When dealing with sickness and disease,

His words were short: Be healed; receive your eyesight. He didn't go into a long prayer.

Many times I will talk with a person, but when we get down to it, the actual ministry is extremely short; it is a command. Why? I believe. There is no difference in how I speak to cancer than how I speak in my daily life. I don't work it up; I am not trying to pump anything up. I am not trying to pull all of the energies together, like the *Death Star* in *Star Wars* does. I am not doing that.

If I talk to a sickness, I have no different feeling about it than I would if I wanted good weather. I tell the weather what to do, and I tell the cancer what to do; there is no difference. I want blessings in my life, so I speak blessings all the time. I don't change. I have removed sickness, disease, and death from my vocabulary.

I speak life, I speak health, and I speak blessings. I make people angry, because I refuse to engage in conversations that somehow exalt sickness or disease. I won't do it. A lot of people tell me what the doctors say and I understand that, but they are operating on limited information. They are operating only on what they can see. The way I operate can change what they can see. I don't get involved in what they say. If you have a doctor's report, that's wonderful, but I am not going to believe that report. I am not saying it is not a fact, I am just saying that I am not going to believe it, because what I believe will come to pass.

Whenever you speak and you say that you believe that your words will come to pass and you shall have whatsoever you say, it is that simple. People can say, "Well, I just don't believe that." That's fine. There were people on one side of the Jordan who said, "I don't believe that is the land of milk and honey. I believe that is the land of giants," and they all died in the wilderness.

You are going to have to make a choice. What are you going to believe? Are you going to believe what man says? In Romans 10:17, it says, "Faith comes by hearing, and hearing by the Word of God." Doubt and unbelief come by hearing the words of man, which are generally the words of Satan. Even if a man is born again, as an un-regenerated or un-renewed man his mind isn't renewed. He still thinks like the devil. That's a fact.

That is why Jesus told Peter, "Get thee behind me Satan, because you savor not the things of God, but of man." He compared man's mind with the devil's mind. I go by what the Word of God says. As I said before, "There is no difference when I am talking to a situation or when I am talking to a cancer; there is no different feeling."

The only time there is a different feeling is when there might be a feeling of compassion for the person I am praying for. That is really the only difference. There is no difference in power, focus, or anything else. I can tell a cancer to go, and I can tell a sickness to go, and to you it might actually sound almost flippant. It is not meant that way. I mean it with the same seriousness, but I don't have to focus in and get serious.

There are times when I enjoy myself and have a good time, but when there is sickness, disease, or any other kind of situation, I am serious about it. I don't have to look serious because it's not my looks that get the job done—it is what is in my heart and what I believe. You can decide to believe in a second.

The next verse says that you have to believe that those things you *say* will come to pass, and you will have whatsoever you *say*.

> *24 Therefore I say unto you, What things soever ye desire, when ye pray, believe that ye receive them, and ye shall have them.*

He was talking about your normal, everyday way of talking. You should never *say* anything that you don't want to come to pass. It is just that simple.

Say what you want to come to pass. Don't say what you have been having. Look ahead, see the end result, and speak that. Verse 24 starts with the word, "Therefore." What does *therefore* mean? Kenneth Hagin used to say, "When you see a *therefore*, find out what it is there for."

"*Therefore*," in verse 24 is there because of verse 23. This has somewhat to do with your answer to unanswered prayer. Some people might ask, "Why aren't my prayers answered?" I am going to give you one of the reasons: it is because you don't believe the *therefore*. You will pray, but you won't realize that praying works. Whatever you *say* will come to pass, and because of that, you can pray. That is what guarantees an answer to your prayer.

He says, "Therefore," because you will have whatever you *say*, whatever you believe, and you will doubt not in your heart. Jesus said, "Therefore, I *say* unto you, what things soever you desire when you pray, believe that ye receive them, and ye shall have them." You will have what you *say* when you pray. Believe that you receive those things, and you shall have them.

What does that mean? It will change the way you pray.

This does not say that you have to beg God for something. It says that you shall believe in your heart that what you *say* will come to pass, and because of that, when you pray, you are *saying* what you want to come to pass. You believe that you receive them, because you receive what you *say*. Once you *say* it to God and you have believed, then at that point, you can only *say* that you received. You can't say that you don't have it.

The beauty is that at that point, you still don't see it because you have only said it. First you *say* it, and then you will see it. You shouldn't necessarily expect to see it right when you *say* it. I am not saying that you shouldn't believe for instant answers to prayers. It could happen the second after you *say* it. However, the second you *say* it, you don't have it or you wouldn't have said it.

You *say* what you want to come to pass. You don't say, "Oh, God, do you see this sick person and their problems? God, help them with their problems." What do you think He has been doing? He has been helping them with their problems. That's why they came to you so that you could help them out of their problems. He has already been helping them, and you are trying to beg Him into doing it. "Oh, God, don't you care? Don't you see what they're going through?" God knows all of that; He knew that before you got up that morning. You have to automatically know this.

Because you are *in* Christ and He is *in* you, and you and the Father are one as He and the Father are one, you have been granted an audience with God. You don't have to go to Jerusalem; you don't even have to go to your prayer closet. God's presence is with you, so anything you *say*, you are saying in the presence of God. When you are speaking, know that He will hear you and that He will answer your prayers.

It's as if He says, "What do you want?" and you say, "I am so sick. God, you don't understand. It's horrible; my problems are just so bad." He didn't ask, "What problems are you having?" He asked, "What do you want?" He didn't say, "Tell me how it's been." He knows how it's been. He says, "Tell Me what you want Me to do. What do you want?" You say, "I want cancer to go!" God says, "Now, I know what you want, so I agree. Cancer, get out!"

That is the way real prayer works. It is when you start speaking the end result, knowing that God hears your prayers. Isn't that what Jesus said at Lazarus' tomb?

They came together and they said, "Lord, if you had only been here, he wouldn't have died, but even now we know that whatever you ask of God, He will give it to you."

Jesus looked at them and said, "Don't you understand that he will rise up in the resurrection?" "Oh, we know he will rise up in the resurrection." Jesus said, "I am the Resurrection. You are not waiting on anything. I am here."

That's the problem with most Christians; they still have that mindset. You are not waiting on anything. God is with you. Jesus is with you. He is the Resurrection, the Truth, and the Life. All of that is there. He is with you, right now. You just need to speak that out.

Jesus said, "The only reason I am praying is because of these people." He said, "Father, I thank you for hearing Me, and I know You always hear Me. I am just praying so that these people will know that We are connected." There was no reason for Him to say very much; there was no reason for Him to pray.

Think about this: He was praying and Lazarus was still in the tomb. Lazarus wasn't even moving. Lazarus didn't move until Jesus said, "Lazarus, come forth." He could have skipped all of that praying and just have gone right to "Lazarus, come forth!" and Lazarus would still have come forth. The only reason He prayed was so that people would hear Him pray and know that God was with Him. That is the only reason you need to pray, especially about sickness or disease or anything that has been included in the Atonement.

If only I could get this across to some people! Many times people will write to me but usually they will call. They will call and say, "I have to get through to Brother Curry. I have to talk to him." I will get the message, and I will ask, "What is this about?" They will say, "It is about this person who has this disease, and all of these things have been going on. They want to talk to you."

As soon as I read that, I don't even have to pray. I am not saying I don't pray, but I am saying I don't have to pray about that. What I have to do is believe. The praying doesn't bring the answer; believing brings the answer. When I see that, I have to mentally focus on it, because we are three parts: spirit, soul, and body.

I look at that situation, and at that moment, I make a decision to believe that the Word of God is true for that person. I just look at it and say, "The Word of God is true. By His stripes they were healed in Jesus' name (Isaiah 53:5, 1 Peter 2:24, Matthew 8:16, 17)." It is not a matter of praying; it is a matter of believing.

The people who call think that nothing will happen until I call them back. However, by the time I call them, I have already started speaking to the thing, and the Spirit of God is already at work. I have already said, "In the name of Jesus, be healed." Why? That's because I am speaking to that thing. It doesn't say to speak to the person with the problem. It says speak to the problem, so I speak to the problem before I ever speak to the person. As a matter of fact, I don't even have to speak to the person. I can speak to the problem that is bothering the person, and the problem will have to obey and do what I tell it to do.

If you get hold of this, life will get so much easier than just being religious and thinking you have to say the perfect incantation prayer over a person perfectly, every time. Religious people think that they have to be in the presence of the person or have to be on the phone with them. They don't have to do any of that.

Do you remember the Roman centurion's servant who was healed by Jesus from a distance? We don't know anything about him. For all we know, he didn't even tell the servant. He might have said, "I am going to go and see if I can find this Jesus and get this thing taken care of." He might have said something like that, but for all we know, maybe he just found out that his servant was sick and about to die, and he said, "I am going to go and get help."

The Roman centurion went to Jesus and said, "My servant is sick." Jesus said, "I will come and heal him." He said, "No, you don't have to come to my house. I understand authority. You tell it to go, and it will obey you." He didn't say, "Come to my house and lay hands on the man, because I know how it works." He didn't say any of that. He said, "Just tell it to go."

Jesus never told the sickness to go. He just said, "This is great faith!" He turned to His own disciples and said, "What's the matter with you guys? I haven't found this kind of faith in any of you, and this guy is a Roman centurion." He then turned back around to the centurion and talked about his great faith. Astonished at his faith, Jesus said, "Go your way. It will be done even as you have said; so be it." That was it. He was talking to the man, and the thing had to obey.

Think about that. We limit God so much to routines and formulas, and God is so much bigger than formulas. When my children need something from me, they don't have to put in a requisition in writing and send it through the proper channels. They come through my door or they call me and say, "Dad, I need this," and they know they are going to get it. I am trying my best to do for my kids the way God would do for them so that they can see God in how I treat them.

I hope they are getting faith in God by how I answer their requests. I want them to say, "I know if I ask my earthly Dad, he will give it to me, so I know if I ask my heavenly Dad, He will give it to me." This is what I am trying to do. This is also what I try to do with my staff. I make it so that I lead by example. I don't always live up to it, I'm sure, but I'm trying.

I want you to realize what faith does. You can have faith in God because God keeps His promises. His Word is true. We are people of faith; we're born of faith. Look again at what He said in verse 24:

> 24 Therefore I say unto you, What things soever ye desire, when ye pray, believe that ye receive them, and ye shall have them.

"Therefore, you will have whatever you desire, when you pray (*say*)." What things shall you have? "What things soever you desire when you pray." It is not when you see them. "You pray (*say*), and believe that you receive them, and you shall have them." In verse 23, He told them: "Doubt not in your heart."

Let's look at how faith works:

You must believe that what you *say* will come to pass.

You must believe and not doubt.

You must look at the desired end and believe that it has been granted, then act and talk like it has been granted.

What does *not doubt* mean? It means *to not waver, hesitate or over analyze a situation.* This is where most Christians fall short. This is where they mess up, and they over analyze. They think too much.

I was watching a healing service the other day. It was amazing because in Africa, if you give a call saying, "If you need healing, come," they will literally run down to the front. They will push and shove to get in line to get you to lay hands on them. There is such an expectation, that they will run down when you make the call. They have to have it organized or people will get crushed.

In America, if you do the same thing, it's like: "Well, I don't know." "Yes, come down front." "Well, I've already got the doctor's appointment, so I don't know.

I could use a blessing, I guess. I'll come down. Did he say any particular disease?" They go through all of these motions. "If I go down, am I going to fall down? I don't want to fall down. I'll get healed; I just don't want to fall." All of these thoughts are going on, and they over-think it.

The thing with the people in Africa is that it's Bam! Bam! Bam! Miracles happen! In America, half the time, you're trying to give it away. It's like somebody standing here saying, "Here's a $100 bill. Who wants it?" "Well, are you sure it's a real $100 bill? I'm not sure it's real; it could be. Are there any strings attached? There have to be strings attached somewhere." That is the way Americans think, but when you go to Africa and say, "Here's a $100 bill," it's out of your hand and you wonder where it went. I mean, it's gone. We wonder and ask, "Why don't we see those things here? We always hear about it in Africa."

Start acting like the Africans. One thing I have learned is that if you want something that somebody else is getting, go and act like they act, and you'll usually get what they got. That can be good or bad. You need to be ready to get hold of this thing, and you need to realize that when something is offered, you need to grab it.

Steve Hill used to say, "The opportunity of a lifetime must be seized during the lifetime of the opportunity." There are literally moments in time that only come around once in a lifetime.

We have put out the call for people to come here and get involved. We have launched hundreds of ministries now around the world and we have said, "Come here and work with us. We are going to establish here, in the Dallas area, a work that is going to demonstrate the power of God. It's going to show how big God is; it is going to show how good God is. There are going to be miracles, and healings, and things taking place that Azusa Street and those early revivals are not going to be able to stand up to in comparison."

You ask, "How can you say that?" That's because the path of the righteous grows brighter and brighter unto the perfect day (Proverbs 4:18). The latter is going to be greater than the former.

I have put that call out, and you would think that there would be standing room only and people lined up down the street. People ask, "Well, what makes me think it will really happen? Can't I do that here?" Sure, you can. You can go and do it there, or you can work together with us to watch what God wants done.

There are some things going on in other places, but God wants things done here in the Dallas area.

Remember what we said about how faith works: you must believe that what you say will come to pass, and you must believe and not doubt, waver, hesitate, or over analyze the situation.

James 1:6-8,

> 6 *But let him ask in faith, nothing wavering. For he that wavereth is like a wave of the sea driven with the wind and tossed.*

> 7 *For let not that man think that he shall receive any thing of the Lord.*

> 8 *A double minded man is unstable in all his ways.*

How do you ask? You ask in faith. You don't hope or wish. How do you ask in faith? Believe that you receive. "Ask in faith, nothing wavering. For he that wavers is like a wave of the sea driven with the wind and tossed. For let not that man think that he shall receive anything of the Lord." You don't hesitate, you don't back off, and you don't waver. If you do, you will receive nothing of the Lord.

In Mark 11:23, it said not to doubt in your heart; it did not say not to doubt in your head. Don't doubt in your heart. You can have ideas going through your head and still not have doubt in your heart. Believe it or not, there are questions that I have about situations and different things, and even about Bible verses, but I do not doubt in my heart.

I have already made the decision; whatever the Word of God says is true. My experiences haven't always lined up with it, but I do not doubt in my heart; I just have questions. It's okay to have questions, just don't let the questions become a doubt in your heart. Choose to believe the Word of God and you will get answers. "A double minded man is unstable in all his ways."

Another thing about how faith works is that you must look at the desired end and believe that it has been granted, then act and talk like it has been granted.

People will think you are crazy when you start living this life, because you are not going to be in step with everybody else. Whatever direction they are going in or whatever they are saying, you are going to be saying the opposite. The world generally goes in the opposite direction of where God want us to go. This may also be true in some of the churches.

There may be people who go to church who are going the opposite way of God, but they are religious, and they are just going through the motions. If you start speaking faith on the Word of God, you will be going in the opposite direction. They will look at you and say, "Who does he think he is?" It's not about who you think you are; it's about who the Bible says you are.

People will not understand that you will have what you *say*. Have faith in God.

Say it with me: "Have faith in God." Now, say, "I have faith in God. I have faith in God, because He keeps His promises." I am skipping to the middle of 2 Corinthians chapter 4, so you might want to go back and read the previous verses.

2 Corinthians 4:10-18,

> *10 Always bearing about in the body the dying of the Lord Jesus, that the life also of Jesus might be made manifest in our body.*

Even though you go through things, His life is made manifest in your body.

11 For we which live are alway delivered unto death for Jesus' sake, that the life also of Jesus might be made manifest in our mortal flesh.

It doesn't say in your immortal flesh, your glorified flesh, but He wants His life living through your mortal flesh, right now.

12 So then death worketh in us, but life in you.

This is the point I wanted to get to:

13 We having the same spirit of faith, according as it is written, I believed, and therefore have I spoken; we also believe, and therefore speak;

It says, "We having the same spirit of faith." Do you realize that faith is a spirit? All men don't have faith. If you're not born again, you don't have faith. Now you can have things out of the soul, you can have desires, and you can have positive thinking, but positive thinking isn't faith. Positive thinking, technically speaking, is a counterfeit faith. It's the natural, fallen man's faith.

The Bible says that not all men have faith, but if you are born again, you have faith. If you have been born again, you have received the measure of faith; it is not *a* measure, but *the* measure. We all have the same measure of faith. You can develop your faith. We were all born with the same amount of muscles, but you can develop the muscles or you can let them atrophy. Most people's faith muscles have atrophied. You have to start exercising them and build them up.

I am so glad for the Word of God. Even though I have read it through, front to back, several hundred times now, it is always fresh; it is always alive. Last night, I sat down and started writing these things out and putting them together, and I got so excited! The Word of God was alive! I was reading it aloud, speaking it out. When I am writing these, I read them out, and I speak them out loud.

I was talking to God, angels, demons, devils, and whoever else was around me, because I wanted them all to hear it. I started reading this, and it was just like fanning coals; it just burst into a flame! It was like, "Lord, I have got to find something I can use faith on! I've got to use faith on something!"

I was in the office until close to 9 p.m. last night, and I had to get up and start walking around. I started cleaning the office, trying to get things put up, because the office is not all put together yet. I am trying to fix things up a bit. I was putting things by the door to load into my SUV, so I could take them home and get them out of the office. I kept looking at the clock and thinking, "I need to go home and get back, but I am so pumped that is almost like I am wired." I was trying to think about prayer requests that I had gotten so I could just hit those things.

I was walking around back there, cleaning, and praying in tongues a little bit, but mostly I was just meditating on what I had been reading. I pulled my vehicle around, and I put everything that was at the back door into it. I was just about to turn out the lights and leave, but I was still pumped, and I was looking for something to exercise my faith on.

My office goes out to an alley, and I had the door open. I never just leave that door standing open, but this time I did, and I heard this car coming through. It was late at night, so I wanted to see who was driving through the alley. Even though all of this isn't our building, I still want to know who is driving through the alley. I stepped out to look, and there was a car going by on the other side of the SUV, so I really couldn't see anybody.

I turned around and started to walk back in, and as I turned, I heard a lady's voice saying, "Brother Curry, Brother Curry." I turned around and walked back out the door and the lady pulled past my SUV to where I could see her. I said, "Yes?" and I walked up to the car. She rolled down her window, told me her name, and said that she had just flown in from Florida. It was then that I heard a baby in the back. She said, "I flew here with my son; I have my baby here." I said, "I know; I hear him."

She said, "I have been trying to get hold of you. I have sent emails and I have called. I couldn't get in touch with you, so I just got on a plane and flew here. My husband stayed in Florida with our other kids, and here I am. You have got to pray for my baby."

I said, "Okay, pull up over here, and bring your baby inside." She got the baby out of the car and brought him in, and we sat on the couch back there. I took the baby and ministered to him. I said, "Okay, we will see you tomorrow."

It didn't take any time at all. Most of our time was spent just talking, and that was like five minutes. The ministry to the child was maybe a minute. It was a four-month-old baby who needed help. As soon as she left, I got my keys, headed out the door and was ready to leave. I realized I was still pumped, and the need to exercise my faith on something wasn't gone, but it was satisfied. I don't stay up here late every night, especially not on a Saturday night, but God arranged it.

That woman had been praying. She said that her whole flight there she was praying, "God, let him come into work today. Let him be there tonight." She thought, "Should I drive by there at 8 o'clock on a Saturday night?" That was God. She had faith in God, I had faith in God, and all we had to do was get together. It was a divine appointment.

If you had asked me five minutes before, I wouldn't have thought there was going to be a divine appointment. I was just looking for something to use my faith on. When you want to use your faith, God will find something for you to use your faith on. How many of you know that that baby was healed? God didn't orchestrate all of that just to leave that baby not healed.

Let's read that verse again:

> *13 We having the same spirit of faith, according as it is written, I believed, and therefore have I spoken; we also believe, and therefore speak;*

He says, "We having the same *spirit of faith*, according as it is written, I believed and therefore have I spoken." Isn't it amazing that all of these things are right here in the same verse? Having the same spirit of faith, the Word (according as it is written), believe, and speaking are in one verse. If you want the divine chemical analysis of faith, that's it, right there.

He said, "We also believe, and therefore speak." If you have faith in God, you will speak. Notice that the *spirit of faith* is connected with the written Word of God and the speaking.

> *14 Knowing that he which raised up the Lord Jesus shall raise up us also by Jesus, and shall present us with you.*

To have the *spirit of faith*, you must know something.

> *15 For all things are for your sakes, that the abundant grace might through the thanksgiving of many redound to the glory of God.*

> *16 For which cause we faint not; but though our outward man perish, yet the inward man is renewed day by day.*

> *17 For our light affliction, which is but for a moment, worketh for us a far more exceeding and eternal weight of glory;*

This was the apostle Paul writing. He said, "For our light affliction (problem), will work an exceeding weight of glory." We find out in the next verse when it will work that exceeding weight of glory.

18 While we look not at the things which are seen, but at the things which are not seen: for the things which are seen are temporal; but the things which are not seen are eternal.

"For our light affliction (problem), will work an exceeding weight of glory while we look not at the things which are seen, but at the things which are not seen."

People say, "Well, God did this to make me a better person." The only way that this could be true is if they are not looking at the problem but are looking at the unseen. He tells us, "While we look not at the things which are seen, but we look at the things which are not seen." How can we look at things which are not seen?

That is exactly the first thing I asked and God said, "The only place where you can look at unseen things is in the Word of God. Look at what has been written." What He has written down is unseen, as of yet. You look at the unseen, and words create pictures, so when you read the Word, you are seeing the unseen. When you look at the unseen, the things you can see will change to match the unseen.

The only time your problem benefits you is when you quit looking at the problem and start looking at the Word of God which gives you the answer for the problem. You say as He says, "We have the same spirit of faith, therefore we speak." When you see the answer and you believe the answer, you will start to speak the answer. Then, what you see in reality is the answer.

The unseen becomes the seen and replaces the seen and makes the seen, unseen. It might take a little time for you to go through it. The only place that you can see the unseen is in the Word of God, "For the things which are seen are temporal; but the things which are not seen are eternal."

Have faith in God. His Word is true. Notice: God is working in you and through you, and He is working with you. Have faith in God. He is *in* you. He's working with you, and He's working *in* you. He's with you, *in* you, and working through you. You've got to get that.

2 Corinthians 6:1,

> *1 We then, as workers together with him, beseech you also that ye receive not the grace of God in vain.*

We are co-workers with God; we work together with Him. God has His part, and we have our part.

Hebrews 13:6,

> 6 So that we may boldly say, The Lord is my
> helper, and I will not fear what man shall do
> unto me.

"So that we may boldly say, 'The Lord is my helper.'"
It doesn't say we are His helper—He is our helper. He
is working in you, through you, and with you to help
you do His will.

I know I am giving you a lot of Scripture, but that is
because you are going to have to put all of these things
together.

John 14:12-19,

> 12 Verily, verily, I say unto you, He that believeth
> on me, the works that I do shall he do also; and
> greater works than these shall he do; because I
> go unto my Father.

> 13 And whatsoever ye shall ask in my name, that
> will I do, that the Father may be glorified in the
> Son.

Jesus was saying, "Absolutely, without a doubt, I say
unto you." It doesn't just say I am thinking about you.
He said, "I say unto you, He that believeth on me, the
works that I do shall he do also; and greater works

than these shall he do; because I go unto my Father." He was saying that we would be doing the same works and greater works, and that was because He was going to His Father. Just as sure as Jesus went to the Father, it is just as sure that we can do the same works and greater.

The word, *and,* is a conjunction which means that it ties in with the previous verse. He said, "*And* whatsoever you shall ask in My Name, that will I do, that the Father may be glorified in the Son." He answers your prayers so that the Father can be glorified in the Son. Maybe now you won't try to twist God's arm in order to get Him to do things. Most of the time, it is as if you are fighting with Him or struggling with Him to get Him to do what you ask. He wants to do it, because He wants to receive glory through His Son.

14 If ye shall ask any thing in my name, I will do it.

Here He says it again. How adamant can He be here? He's already said it once. He said, "Whatever you ask in My Name, that will I do, so that the Father can receive glory through the Son." He repeats Himself and says, "If you ask anything in My Name, I will do it." In verse 15, He says,

15 If ye love me, keep my commandments.

Did you know that Jesus gets His prayers answered?

> *16 And I will pray the Father, and he shall give you another Comforter, that he may abide with you for ever;*

That was a promise.

> *17 Even the Spirit of truth; whom the world cannot receive, because it seeth him not, neither knoweth him: but ye know him; for he dwelleth with you, and shall be in you.*

Why can't the world receive the Spirit? It is because, "It sees Him not." The world cannot receive Him, because the world doesn't know how to operate by faith. It doesn't realize that you have to receive Him, and then you will see Him. He was saying, "The world doesn't know Him, but you know Him because He dwells with you, and He shall be *in* you."

> *18 I will not leave you comfortless: I will come to you.*

> *19 Yet a little while, and the world seeth me no more; but ye see me: because I live, ye shall live also.*

He said, "I will not leave you comfortless: I will come to you." He had just said, "The Father will send you another Comforter, the Holy Spirit, and He will abide with you forever." Then He said, "The Spirit dwells with you, and shall be *in* you." He was saying, "You will never be alone again."

Just because you are alone doesn't mean you have to be lonely, because you are never truly alone. He is with you in every situation; He is always there. His wisdom, His power, and everything you need is always there. You can never be farther from God than your desire to know the answer He has for you; He is that close.

He said, "Whatsoever ye shall ask in My Name, that will I do." There is not even an idea that it won't happen. Whatever you ask, He will do it. Why? It is so that the Father can be glorified in the Son. Have faith in God. He always keeps His promises. There is not one thing that He has not fulfilled. You can trust Him, and you can rely upon Him. You can have faith in Him that He will do what He has said He will do.

Matthew 24:35,

> *35 Heaven and earth shall pass away, but my words shall not pass away.*

"My words shall not pass away." Even though heaven and earth will pass away, His Word will remain. The very earth can fall out from under your feet, but if you are standing on His Word, you will stand.

Even if your whole world falls apart, you stand on His word. Your house will remain, as He said, because it is built on the Rock. You can have faith in God. The thing is that you have got to choose to have faith in God. Now, I can have faith that can help you, but there will come a time when you are not around any other humans, and you are going to have to stand on your own faith in God.

As I told you before, the saddest story I have ever heard was about John Lake's son, Roderick. When he was 17 years old, he was lying in a death bed. This was two years after John Lake had died. He said, "I know that if my father were here, I would not have to die." He knew that God heard his father's prayers, but for some reason, it didn't translate down to him. I am telling you, the most miserable thing is to be surrounded by people who have faith and you not get it. It is a sad thing for you to have it at your disposal, for it to be all around you, and yet you don't enter in.

We can read about the different people who did this. We know of Lot's wife. When they were about to be rescued and they were leaving, she was told, "Don't look back." She looked back, and she stayed right there. As she turned, the Bible says that she was turned into a pillar of salt. She was Lot's wife, she saw the angels, she saw the angels rescue them, and she saw everything coming down. She saw the city falling apart, and yet she looked back. Why? It was because her heart was still there.

Listen: you can be around faith, you can hear it, but you've got to get into it. You've got to enter into it by yourself; you've got to push into the things of God and say, "I love my family, but I am getting this. If they don't want to go this way, I can't force them, but I am not going to stop. I am going to get this. I am going to study the Word of God; I am going to live in the Word of God until the Word of God lives and abides *in* me. When I live *in* Him, and He lives *in* me, and His word abides *in* me, and I abide *in* Him, then I can ask whatsoever I will, and it shall be done."

Do you realize that you don't do anybody any good by holding back with them? You do much better by pushing on in. At least then you will get to a place where you can help them.

Nobody went to Smith Wigglesworth's house, because they didn't like being around him. All he wanted to do was read the Word of God, praise God, and talk about the things of God. Lester Sumrall showed up at his

© 2015 – Curry R. Blake –John G. Lake Ministries

door in a top hat with his umbrella and his newspaper under his arm. Every well-dressed man had a newspaper under his arm at that time. Dr. Sumrall said, "I've come to visit you." Wigglesworth said, "Well, you can come in, but leave that trash outside. Hitler and Mussolini will soon be in hell. I'm not going to read about their trash in my home."

This was the mentality Wigglesworth had; he didn't want it in his house. Why? He said, "In my house we are going to serve God. In my house we're going to the read the Word of God, and we're going to pray."

Dr. Sumrall had to leave the newspaper outside. He said when he came back out, somebody had stolen it. He said, "I don't know what happened to the newspaper, but it disappeared when I was in the house."

You can create an atmosphere in your home so that when sick people walk through the door, they don't get prayed for; they get healed by walking into your home. Why? It is because of your faith in God. That's the way it's supposed to be, but you have to work with the Spirit of God, not work against Him.

The Bible says that people actually wrestle against the Word of God to their own destruction. They try to over analyze, and they try to figure things out. There are some things you don't need to figure out. It's like I said before, "Sometimes we will spend 15 minutes looking for a remote control. We will look all over for it instead of just walking over and pushing the button on the TV." That is the way we have become with the Word of God. You ask, "Well, I know what it says, but what does that mean?" Don't over analyze it. Just read the Word.

However, before you open the Bible, just decide: "Whatever I read is truth. Just because I don't understand it doesn't mean it's not true." There may be some things you don't know yet, but God is the sum total of all wisdom in the universe; and what He says is true. You have to make the decision that even with limited understanding you have enough understanding to read the Bible and agree that it's true. That means you have faith in Him.

Mary asked, "Lord, how shall this be, seeing that I have never known a man?" She didn't say, "Lord it can't be, because I've never know a man." She didn't say that. She just asked, "How?" It's okay to ask how. Don't disagree and say, "Well, that can't happen," just because you don't have enough faith."

You have to shut your mouth and quit cursing yourself. If you are going to say anything, say that you have plenty of faith. Why? That's because if you believe you will have what you *say*, then every time you *say*, you will get more faith. Use it to your advantage. God gave it to you for you to use. He wants you to be able to pray, and whatsoever things you desire when you pray, you will receive. He wants you to have them.

John chapter 14:19-26,

> *19 Yet a little while, and the world seeth me no more; but ye see me: because I live, ye shall live also.*

> *20 At that day ye shall know that I am in my Father, and ye in me, and I in you.*

> *21 He that hath my commandments, and keepeth them, he it is that loveth me: and he that loveth me shall be loved of my Father, and I will love him, and will manifest myself to him.*

People ask, "How can I get the manifestation of God? How can I get the manifestation of the Spirit?" One might answer, "Let's all gather at the altar for the next forty days and fast and pray. We're just going to cry out to God, and God will manifest Himself." It never says to do that. What makes you think that you can dictate to God the requirements that will cause Him to show up?

Do you want to know what makes God show up? The answer is written right in the Word. You have His commandments, and you keep them. If you do that, it proves you love Him, and if you love Him, you will be loved of Him. He says, "And I will love him and will manifest myself to him." Do you want to see the manifestation of the Spirit of God? It's easy. Keep His commandments, love Him, be loved of Him, and He will manifest Himself. Isn't that simple?

It doesn't say that you have to struggle, cry, beat your fists on the floor, and make promises to God that you don't really intend to keep. It doesn't say any of that. His commandments are very simple: love the Lord thy God with all your heart, mind, soul, and strength, and love your neighbor as yourself.

"How do I love my neighbor as myself?" Do to them, what you would have done unto you. This is the commandment you keep; it's that simple. How hard is to love God? It's easy. How hard is to love other people? Okay, I will admit it is sometimes hard, but the more you love God, the more your love for people grows. The more your love for people grows, the more you start to keep those commandments. When you keep those commandments, you love Him, and He loves you, and He manifests himself.

How does He manifest himself? You get to do for others, what you would have done for yourself. You get to lay hands on the sick, and they get healed. If you were sick, you would want somebody to come to you, and that's how He manifests Himself. Do you see how simple this is? We have made this thing into a religion, and God never meant for it to be that. He meant for it to be a relationship.

> *22 Judas saith unto him, not Iscariot, Lord, how is it that thou wilt manifest thyself unto us, and not unto the world?*

> *23 Jesus answered and said unto him, If a man love me, he will keep my words: and my Father will love him, and we will come unto him, and make our abode with him.*

"If a man love Me, he will keep My words." Did you notice that He said it again?

> *24 He that loveth me not keepeth not my sayings: and the word which ye hear is not mine, but the Father's which sent me.*

"He that loveth me not, keepeth not my sayings." This was the third time He said the same thing, but in a different way.

> *25 These things have I spoken unto you, being yet present with you.*

> *26 But the Comforter, which is the Holy Ghost, whom the Father will send in my name, he shall teach you all things, and bring all things to your remembrance, whatsoever I have said unto you*

In other words, "I am not making this up as I go. I am just relaying to you God's promises." This is one of His promises: "These things have I spoken unto you, being yet being present with you, but the Comforter, which is the Holy Ghost, whom the Father will send in my Name, He shall teach you all things, and bring all things to your remembrance, whatsoever I have said unto you."

John 16:7-14,

> *7 Nevertheless I tell you the truth; it is expedient for you that I go away: for if I go not away, the Comforter will not come unto you; but if I depart, I will send him unto you.*

> *8 And when he is come, he will reprove the world of sin, and of righteousness, and of judgment:*

9 Of sin, because they believe not on me;

10 Of righteousness, because I go to my Father, and ye see me no more;

11 Of judgment, because the prince of this world is judged.

12 I have yet many things to say unto you, but ye cannot bear them now.

13 Howbeit when he, the Spirit of truth, is come, he will guide you into all truth: for he shall not speak of himself; but whatsoever he shall hear, that shall he speak: and he will shew you things to come.

14 He shall glorify me: for he shall receive of mine, and shall shew it unto you.

In other words, "The Spirit of truth will teach you. He is not going to speak of Himself, but He will show you things to come." He said, "He shall glorify Me: for He shall receive of Mine, and shall show it unto you."

We are still talking about having faith in God. Faith comes by hearing, and hearing by the Word of God. Hopefully as you read these verses, faith will rise up within you, and you will start to realize: "I can trust Him; I can rely upon Him. He said it, and it shall be."

When you start speaking with that surety, some people are not going to like you. They are not going to like you, because you are sure. This is one of the first things people say to me: "How can you be so sure about this?" I tell them, "Because it's there in the Word of God." Isn't that simple?

Mark 16:19-20,

> *19 So then after the Lord had spoken unto them, he was received up into heaven, and sat on the right hand of God. And they went forth, and preached everywhere, the Lord working with them, and confirming the word with signs following. Amen.*

> *20 And they went forth, and preached everywhere, the Lord working with them, and confirming the word with signs following.*

Notice that the Lord didn't do it by Himself. He worked with His disciples. They preached. They had their part, we have our part, and God has His part. "The Lord was working with them, and confirming the Word with signs following." We are co-workers together. Have faith in God. He will keep His promises.

Philippians 2:12-13,

> *12 Wherefore, my beloved, as ye have always obeyed, not as in my presence only, but now much more in my absence, work out your own salvation with fear and trembling.*

> *13 For it is God which worketh in you both to will and to do of his good pleasure.*

This desire that you have for the things of God that makes you want to do the things of God isn't even you. It is God, *in* you, giving you that desire.

Psalm 37:4,

> *4 Delight thyself also in the LORD; and he shall give thee the desires of thine heart.*

It doesn't mean that He is going to give you what you want. He is going to give you *the want.* He will cause you to want the right things. It is God *in* you giving you both the will to do things and the ability to do them. God doesn't just make you want to do things; He gives you the ability to do the things of God. Have faith in God. What do you need faith in God for? You need faith in God so that He can accomplish His will through your life.

To some people, the biggest hurdle they have to go over is to realize that God could actually accomplish His will through their life, and that he could actually use them to do these things. We talk all the time about how God can do anything. Well, of course we believe that He can, but that is a very general faith. There comes a point when you have to make it a specific faith and say, "God can do this thing."

Most people will say that God can do anything, but when it comes down to it, you start to find out what they believe. People will say, "Well, God can't do that. There are just some things God can't do." They don't get it.

We have to be able to take His general promise and apply it to a specific problem. God gives us the desire to do what He wants done, and then He gives us the Holy Spirit to help us, or empower us, to do the very thing that He desires to do through us.

John 14:10,

> *14 Believest thou not that I am in the Father, and the Father in me? the words that I speak unto you I speak not of myself: but the Father that dwelleth in me, he doeth the works.*

"The Father that dwells *in* me, He does the works."

Galatians 2:20,

> *20 I am crucified with Christ: nevertheless I live; yet not I, but Christ liveth in me: and the life which I now live in the flesh I live by the faith of the Son of God, who loved me, and gave himself for me.*

"It is no longer I who live, but Christ Who lives *in* me."

Philippians 4:13,

> *13 I can do all things through Christ which strengthens me.*

What was Paul saying here? He had just talked about the things he had gone through. He wasn't necessarily talking about healing the sick. He was talking about shipwrecks, and being hungry, and going through all of these problems. He said, "But I can do all things." In other words, "I can do this; I am not going to quit." Why? "It is because I can do all things through Christ who strengthens me." He was saying, "I can persevere, and I can overcome all obstacles to accomplish God's will."

You need to have faith in God. You need to decide: "I can do this. He put the desire in me and gave me the ability, and now He's *in* me and working through me.

I can do all things, through Christ, who strengthens me. I have faith in Him, that He will keep His Word."

It's not about how much faith you have. It's that you have faith in Him, that He will keep His Word. Your faith is not in your faith; your faith is in God. Have faith in God.

Daniel 11:32,

> *32 But the people that do know their God shall be strong, and do exploits.*

If you know God, then you should be doing exploits. Exploits of what? Exploits of faith. You should be looking for ways to believe God and areas to believe God in. You should be looking for things to apply your faith toward, so you can bring glory to God. In that way you say, "I believe Him. I believe God."

Isn't this what Paul said? He said, "If we go on this trip, there is going to be a shipwreck. It is going to be bad, but I believe God. The angel of the Lord stood by me tonight and told me that we're going to be okay. I believe God." Everybody on the ship was saved because Paul believed God.

Joel 3:10,

> *10 Beat your plowshares into swords, and your pruninghooks into spears: let the weak say, I am strong.*

It says, "Let the weak say, 'I am strong.'" The time to have faith in God is now. The minute you believe, it becomes real to you.

Paul prayed under the inspiration of the Holy Spirit in Ephesians chapter one.

Ephesians 1:17-23,

> *17 That the God of our Lord Jesus Christ, the Father of glory, may give unto you the spirit of wisdom and revelation in the knowledge of him.*
>
> *18 The eyes of your understanding being enlightened; that you may know what is the hope of his calling, and what the riches of the glory of his inheritance in the saints.*

Paul was praying for the people saying, "May God give you the spirit of wisdom and revelation in the knowledge of Him." You already have the Spirit of God. You already know that in Christ is hidden all the treasures of wisdom, so you have the spirit of wisdom. You have the spirit of understanding, and that spirit will teach you, and guide you, and lead you into all things. You need to understand that.

You have all of that. Why do you have it? "That you may know what is the hope of His calling." You have it so that you can know what you are supposed to be doing and how you are supposed to be living.

Paul prayed, "May the eyes of your understanding being enlightened; that you may know what are the riches of the glory of his inheritance in the saints." You already have the inheritance in the saints and all of the riches of the glory of God that are in that. You have an inheritance, but it takes faith to get it. Faith is how you receive your inheritance.

What is your inheritance? It's everything in the Bible that is a promise, but it takes faith to believe it. Decide it's true for you, and start to speak like it is true. You will go exactly the opposite direction from the way the world is going. When the world is going toward sickness and disease, you will be going toward health and healing. When the world is screaming about the economy, you will prosper, and you'll be blessed.

> *19 And what is the exceeding greatness of his power to us-ward who believe, according to the working of his mighty power."*

This verse starts with the word, "And," which means that this is an add-on to what Paul was already praying that you would receive. He was praying that we would know how great God's power is toward us. In other words, he wanted us to know how much God has put at our disposal. It is the exact same power that is in verse 20:

> 20 *Which he wrought in Christ, when he raised him from the dead, and set him at his own right hand in the heavenly places. "*

The same degree of power that raised Jesus from the dead is the same degree of power that God has available at your disposal. This is what He has for you; it is that much power. That was the greatest display of power, ever, in the history of the universe. It superseded creation. It superseded everything else because at creation there was no resistance, but to raise Jesus from the dead, there was resistance.

It didn't amount to much in comparison to God, but there was resistance. It says, "Which he wrought in Christ, when he raised him from the dead, and set him at his own right hand in the heavenly places."

> 21 *Far above all principality, and power, and might, and dominion, and every name that is*

named, not only in this world, but also in that which is to come:

22 And hath put all things under his feet, and gave him to be the head over all things to the church.

It was good for Jesus and then it got good for us, because we are seated together with Him in heavenly places. If anything is under Jesus' feet, it's under your feet. Neither principalities, powers, dominions, nor any of those things have authority over you. They are under your feet, and it's up to you to decide to have faith in God and start saying the end result.

To quote Reinhard Bonnke, "Dallas shall be saved." This is what he said about Africa and now he is coming to America. We can say, "Dallas shall be healed. Dallas shall be delivered."

We can say this about any place where we have authority, or anywhere we have influence. You say, "Well, I just can't believe that God can change a city in a day." In a day things can change, but it is going to take us being a people of faith and taking the limits off of God and believing what He can do to change things.

23 And gave him to be the head over all things to the church, which is his body, the fulness of him that filleth all in all.

Think about that: we are the fullness of Him that fills all in all.

Ephesians 3:13-14,

> *13 For this cause I bow my knees unto the Father of our Lord Jesus Christ, of whom the whole family in heaven and earth is named."*

We are all given that name by birth. Here is more of what Paul was praying:

> *14 That he would grant you, according to the riches of his glory, to be strengthened with might by his Spirit in the inner man.*

This is what He desires for you: that your inner man be strengthened. What does that mean? It means that you will say what you expect to come to pass, and you will start to believe the things that God has for you. It means that you will have faith in God, and that you will step out, and that you will know your God, and you will do exploits for Him. Jesus was never meant to be just a life preserver that allows you to float through life. He was meant to empower you, so that you could live His life on this earth. It was meant for Him to live His life through you so that you could do exploits that would bring glory to God.

Ephesians 3:17,

> *17 That Christ may dwell in your hearts by faith; that ye, being rooted and grounded in love, may be able to comprehend with all saints what is the breadth, and length, and depth, and height; and to know the love of Christ, which passeth knowledge, that ye might be filled with all the fulness of God.*

This is amazing: you are supposed to know something that you can't know. "Know the love of Christ which passes knowledge." In other words, you are supposed to know something which goes beyond knowing so that you may be filled with all the fullness of God. This was written for us, so we have got to believe it.

"That we may be *filled...*" What does *filled* mean? I know that may seem simple, but I looked it up. The word *filled* literally means *to be crammed full*. Think about that. You are to be *crammed full* of the fullness of God, Himself. What fills up God? Love is what fills up God, and He uses power to display His love.

We are always full of whatever we eat. We should be eating the Word of God so that the Spirit of God can help us. We should be living in this, and this is what we should be full of. We should be so busy with this that we don't have time for any of the other things. I am not saying that you can't do your job. I am telling you that if you fill yourself with the Word of God, the Spirit of God will use that to work wisdom in your job. You will get more done in less time and without paying nearly as much attention to it. You will prosper at your job, and you will get promoted. That's what God does.

Some people are full of soap operas. If you are full of soap operas, you are probably going to have problems with fantasy and lust. That's just the way it is because that's what soap operas are geared toward. Some people are full of horror films, and they usually have a problem with fear. You get full of whatever you feed off of. Some are full of medical dramas, and they are usually full of doubt and unbelief in the supernatural and supernatural deliverance.

I told you a while back that I like movies that make me think. I always liked *NCIS* with Jethro Gibbs; he is a role model. I also watched a show called *House.* I liked the way it would show the body and what happened to it. It was just very technical. House thinks outside of the box; he thinks differently. That is the part I liked; he thought outside of the box.

House is the name of the Doctor on the show. He has an attitude, and he is pretty ungodly. I was sitting there one night watching *House*. As it moved on, it got more and more atheistic, which is what they do. It is like the frog in the water, and they keep turning up the heat. They think that because you are hooked, you won't turn it off.

As I was sitting there watching this, as clear as day I heard God say, "If you keep watching this, you are going to hurt your faith." I literally stopped, because it was like somebody in the room said it. He said again, "If you keep watching this, you are going to hurt your faith."

Why do you think God told me that? It was because they always had a natural reason and a natural remedy. Do you know what I mean by that? They did not have a supernatural remedy.

I am telling you, as soon as God spoke, I got up, I turned it off, and to this day, I have never watched it again. Why? It is because my faith is more important than 30 minutes of amusement or even mental stimulation of thinking. People's lives depend on my faith. I don't have the luxury of feeding on garbage.

You say, "Well, nobody depends upon my faith." You depend on your faith. "Well, no, that's what I have you for." Then you had better hope that you can get hold of me when you need me. I am not trying to be mean or anything like that, because I try to be available to everybody, but it gets harder and harder as more and more people come in.

The idea is not for me to do it all for you; it is for you to grow up and be able to do it for others. You have got to love God with all your heart, soul, mind, and strength, and love your neighbor as yourself. That means you don't call Brother Curry when you find out the neighbor is sick. It means that you should be able to handle it and come in here on Sunday with a testimony.

Ephesians 3:20,

> *20 Now unto him that is able to do exceeding abundantly above all that we ask or think, according to the power that works in us." How can He do exceeding, abundantly above all we think or ask?*

It's according to the power that works in us, not just the power that is present. There is a difference between potential power and realized power. Potentially, you have the absolute power of God dwelling in you. Whatever God can do is in you right now. That's potential power, but it is you feeding on the Word of God, choosing to have faith, stepping out in the things of God, and deciding to do exploits for

God that will cause that potential power to become realized through your life.

Faith takes risk. You can't have faith and live in comfort. You have to get out of your comfort zone. If you want things to be different from what you have had before, then you have got to do things differently, more differently than you have ever done.

I have told you all the story of how I started doing this. I watched all of the old videos of all of God's Generals, and then I got hold of some tapes by David Hogan. I remember telling my wife, "I am not going to turn 70, sitting in a rocking chair on my front porch, wondering, 'What if?'"

I would rather have jumped out there, tried it, and have absolutely failed than ended up in that chair. Then I could have put it all behind me and gone back to teaching martial arts or whatever else I wanted to do. I would rather have done that, than just played with it all my life and been a person who went to a church that said, "We believe in this."

I decided at that point that I didn't want that. I was in a good church, but there was a lot more excitement there than there was believing. There was a lot more excitement there than there was manifestation.

I made a decision not to go that route and settle into being just a good Christian. I decided that wasn't the idea of Christianity from what I saw in the Bible. I made this decision: I am going to step out. People kept telling me I couldn't. They said all kinds of negative things, so I got away from them. I started doing what the Word of God says, and instead of sitting on my porch when I am 70 saying, "What if?" I will still be going and traveling around the world. I will be able to take time to sit with my grandchildren and show them hundreds of photo albums. I will go through them and say, "See this? This was in Malta, and this was in Italy. This is a person who was dead and is now alive, because we went there and spoke life into him, and he got up.

This was in South Africa. This man was brought in on a stretcher with a blanket, and they said he wouldn't even make it through the service. When I laid hands on him, I started crying. I stood up, and I touched him with my foot and I said, "Get up! Take up your bed and walk." Here are the pictures of him walking off, and he gained weight before the service was over.

I have all of these photo albums. I have been going through these albums in my office. I have 44, so far, that are filled. You say, "Well, a minute ago, you said hundreds." I'm not done yet. I have places to go and things to do. I have exploits out there. There are good works that I was foreordained to walk in. The same things are there for you, so have faith in God. Trust Him. Look for areas where you haven't been trusting in Him, and decide to trust Him. Find the Scriptures or whatever you need. Just trust Him, and step out. Watch and see if He will not be glorified through answering your prayer.

Chapter 3

Manifesting the Spirit of Faith

In this message, we're going to be ministering along the lines of not just having the *spirit of faith* but manifesting the *spirit of faith.* One of the main Scriptures we talked about before was 2 Corinthians 4:13. This is about having the *spirit of faith.*

2 Corinthians 4:13,

> *13 We having the same spirit of faith, according as it is written, I believed, and therefore have I spoken; we also believe, and therefore speak;*

It says, "We having the <u>same</u> *spirit of faith.*" There is a lot you can get out of this one verse. You can go back and read the whole chapter of 2 Corinthians 4. The key here is this: we all have the <u>same</u> *spirit of faith.*

Then he said: "According as it is written..." In other words, it was written down. I want you to notice this about Paul. He said, "It is written, I believed, and therefore have I spoken." Then he said, "We also *believe*, and therefore *speak*." Since we have the <u>same</u>

spirit of faith as the people who were writing the Bible, we *believe*, and we also *speak.*

Paul was saying that what you see in a person in the Bible is what's in you. If it's in them and it's in you, then you can do what they did. Amen? It's not just that you can, but you should, because if they had the *spirit of faith*, and you have the *spirit of faith*, then you ought to be manifesting the *spirit of faith* the way they did. It might not be exactly the same way, but in the same manner. You ought to be able to manifest the *spirit of faith.*

Hebrews 11:6,

> *6 But without faith it is impossible to please him: for he that cometh to God must believe that he is, and that he is a rewarder of them that diligently seek him.*

We are going to lay some groundwork with this Scripture. Everybody knows it: "But without faith it is impossible to please Him." If you don't have faith, you can't please Him. You cannot please God without faith. "For he that cometh to God must believe that He is," that He exists, "and that He is a rewarder of them that diligently seek Him."

There are two things involved in faith.

Number one: you have to believe that God is (that He exists).

Number two: you have to believe that He rewards those who diligently seek Him.

People ask me, "Oh, you believe in divine healing?" No, I don't believe in divine healing. I don't have faith for healing. I believe in God who is the healer. I don't believe in a God who is a healer. People say, "Well I believe in a God who is a healer, I believe in a healing God." I don't say it that way. Why? Because it says, "He is the Lord that healeth thee." I don't believe in any other ways, gods, or anything else. My God has made His name, Jehovah Rapha. That is His Name. He is the God that healeth thee.

Exodus 15:26,

> *26 And said, If thou wilt diligently hearken to the voice of the LORD thy God, and wilt do that which is right in his sight, and wilt give ear to his commandments, and keep all his statutes, I will put none of these diseases upon thee, which I have brought upon the Egyptians: for I am the LORD that healeth thee.*

The word, *healeth*, is in the present tense and is always in the present tense, so the God that heals you is always a present tense God. Not past. Not future. He's not the God that is going to heal you; He's not the God that did heal you. He is the God that heals you, present tense, every day, right now. I can walk in that life and health every second, and when I walk in healing every second, that is called divine health.

This is better than getting sick, getting well, getting sick, and getting well. People say, "Well, do you believe in that faith healing stuff?" No, I don't have faith for healing or in healing. I have faith in God, Who is the Healer. My faith is in God.

My faith is not in healing, because if my faith was in healing and somebody did not get healed, then my faith would falter. My faith is in God, Who is the Healer, and because of that, my faith in healing, in that sense, would never falter. He is *the God that heals you*.

Romans 14:23,

> *23 And he that doubteth is damned if he eat, because he eateth not of faith: for whatsoever is not of faith is sin.*

It says, "Whatsoever is not of faith is sin." When was this written? It was after the crucifixion and resurrection of Christ, and it was written by Paul to the Romans. Apparently, Paul believed that sin still existed after Jesus was resurrected, contrary to common, popular, modern theology that says that there is no sin now. He said, "Whatever is not of faith is sin."

2 Corinthians 4:13,

> *13 We having the same spirit of faith, according as it is written, I believed, and therefore have I spoken; we also believe, and therefore speak;*

Notice what was written here: "We having therefore the same *spirit of faith*." Then it said, "I *believed*, and therefore have I *spoken*; we also *believe*, and therefore *speak*."

Look at the words written: *believed and spoken, believe* and *speak*. Notice what is connected with *believing – speaking*. Every time somebody mentions *believing, speaking* is mentioned with it.

If you have the *spirit of faith*, the number one manifestation of the *spirit of faith* is speaking. You can't get around that; that's just the way it is. The only manifestation of the *spirit of faith* mentioned in the section talking about the *spirit of faith* is speaking. He was saying, "Because I *believe*, I *speak*." If you *believe*, you will *speak*.

Matthew 17:20,

> *20 And Jesus said unto them, Because of your unbelief: for verily I say unto you, If ye have faith as a grain of mustard seed, ye shall say unto this mountain, Remove hence to yonder place; and it shall remove; and nothing shall be impossible unto you.*

On the Mount of Transfiguration, Moses and Elijah appeared in a vision, and they were talking with Jesus. Peter, James, and John said, "Let's build three different tabernacles right here," but Jesus said, "Don't worry about that; that's not what we are here for."

When they came down from the Mount of Transfiguration, they came upon the disciples. The disciples were arguing amongst themselves, but they were also talking about what was going on.

This man had brought his son to the disciples, and the disciples could not set the boy free. After it was all said and done, Jesus said, "Bring the boy to me," and they did. He set the boy free, proving that it was

God's will, even though the disciples couldn't get it done.

Someone might say, "Well, it must not be God's will, if that's what happened in church. They prayed and it didn't happen, so it must not be God's will." The actions or the results of a disciple do not always exemplify the actions or the will of God. Sometimes the disciples don't fulfill the will of God. We know that, because immediately afterward, Jesus set the boy free, so we know it was God's will to set the boy free. Their failure wasn't God's will.

We know that to be the case because they came and asked, "Why couldn't we do it?" Jesus said unto them in verse 20: "Because of your unbelief." End of story. It was that simple. They couldn't do it because of their unbelief.

He said, "Verily I *say*…" Isn't that a form of the word *speak*? "Verily I *say* unto you, if you have faith as a grain of mustard seed you shall *say*…" What does He say? "If you have faith, you shall *say*…" Isn't that what He was saying right there? If you *believe*, you will *speak*. Why? That is how you manifest the *spirit of faith*.

"If you have faith as a grain of mustard seed, you shall *say* unto this mountain, remove hence to yonder place;

and it shall remove." Now, let's look at the second part there: you are going to talk to the mountain, you are going to speak to it, and the mountain is going to obey you.

You are going to command it. Notice, He didn't say, "Mountain, please move." He didn't say, "Father, please move the mountain." He spoke to the mountain and said, "Remove hence to yonder place; and it shall remove; and nothing shall be impossible unto you."

Jesus said here, "If you have faith as a grain of mustard seed..." Jesus never really talked about volume or the amount of faith, but if He had, the amount of faith that will move a mountain is the size of a grain of mustard seed.

Daniel 11:32,

> *32 And such as do wickedly against the covenant shall he corrupt by flatteries: but the people that do know their God shall be strong, and do exploits.*

It says, "And such as do wickedly," and then it changes. We are going to focus on part B of this verse. There is really no way to get around this: "The people who do know God shall be strong, and do exploits." If you know God, you will be strong, and you will do exploits. What it really comes down to is what you consider an exploit.

I am just laying the foundation with some of these Scriptures. In Romans chapter 12, Paul was writing to the Romans.

Romans 12:1-3,

> *1 I beseech you therefore, brethren, by the mercies of God, that ye present your bodies a living sacrifice, holy, acceptable unto God, which is your reasonable service.*

> *2 And be not conformed to this world: but be ye transformed by the renewing of your mind, that ye may prove what is that good, and acceptable, and perfect, will of God.*

> *3 For I say, through the grace given unto me, to every man that is among you, not to think of himself more highly than he ought to think; but to think soberly, according as God hath dealt to every man the measure of faith.*

Beseech is a strong word. In other words, "I am urging you; I am really trying to draw this out of you with everything that's in me." Notice: he said, "*You.*" He didn't say God is going to make you present your body. He said, "*You* present your body," so who's presenting your body? *You* present your body a living sacrifice.

Why would you present your body as a living sacrifice?

Many times in church, we talk about the body. Those who don't believe in healing look at the body and say, "Well, healing is just on the far spectrum of things; the important thing is the spirit." Well, absolutely the spirit is important, because that's the real you, and as Paul said, "The flesh is your earthly tent," so your body is important. As soon as your body stops to function, you don't stick around. It's important that your body get fixed whenever it is broken.

Notice what he said in verse 1: "…that ye present your bodies a living sacrifice, holy, acceptable unto God." He was saying, "We are to present our bodies as living sacrifices and present them as holy." Our bodies are to be holy. You are to present your body a living sacrifice, holy unto God.

1 Corinthians 6:19,

> *19 What? know ye not that your body is the temple of the Holy Ghost which is in you, which ye have of God, and ye are not your own?*

Your body, your physical fleshly body, is the temple of the Holy Ghost. You need to realize that your body is holy, and you need to treat it as such.

Romans 12:2,

> *19 And be not conformed to this world: but be ye transformed by the renewing of your mind, that ye may prove what is that good, and acceptable, and perfect, will of God.*

It says, "And be not conformed to this world." We are not to be in this world's system, this world's way of doing things. It says: "...but be transformed." That word *transformed* used there is the same word used about Jesus on the Mount of Transfiguration. It is *metamorphia,* and it literally means *to be changed from the inside out.*

He was saying, "Don't let the world squeeze you into a shape where you act, talk, and look like it. Instead, be transformed from the inside out and let what is in you be seen on the outside." Before it can be seen on the outside, before the Spirit of God can truly live on the outside of you, you have to present your bodies a holy, living sacrifice.

For Him to live through your body, your body has to be dedicated to Him. How are you transformed? How is your body transformed? How is your life transformed? The transformation comes by the renewing of your mind. Renew it to what? Renew it to what the Word of God says.

The Word of God agrees with the new you, which is born again in your spirit. Whenever your mind agrees with your spirit, then your body, which you have already presented as a living sacrifice, makes everything start to line up. People start to see the Spirit of God working through you in every aspect of your life. He says in Romans 12:2, "Be transformed by the renewing of your mind so that you can prove what is the good, acceptable, and perfect will of God."

Watch what he said in Romans 2:3: "For I say…" There he was *saying* again. He said: "…through the grace given unto me, to every man." It says every man, but you know that it means women too, every man and woman – to every person. He said: "For I say, to every man that is among you." What he was *saying*, he was *saying* to everybody; it wasn't just a few. It was to whosoever. He said, "For I *say* to every man that is among you, not to think of himself more highly than he ought to think; but to think soberly, according as God hath dealt to every man the measure of faith." Paul was writing to people in Rome, and he was saying, "Some of you are doing some faith exploits; some things are happening and good things are going on."

The book of Romans is probably the most theological book. These people were thinkers; they were going into these things, and they were sorting them out. He said, "Listen: you have men there who are saying, 'I've got all of this faith, and you haven't got any faith.'"

That's exactly the way it was with the group I used to be with. Someone might say, "Well, I'm not feeling well." "What's the matter with you? Don't you have any faith? Where's your faith?" They were looked down upon if they got sick, and because of that, people started hiding when they got sick. They couldn't talk about it, couldn't ask for help, because that showed a lack of faith.

It got to be where it was very demeaning, and soon, people wouldn't come to church when they were sick, because they didn't want anybody to know that they didn't have faith. That's the way they thought of it, so they just stayed home and suffered instead of actually finding out what needed to be done to live in life and health, and going to church, and getting ministered to.

Of course it wouldn't have mattered back then if they had come to church, because they would have heard,

"Well, if you have faith you will get healed," or "I will pray for you, but if you don't have faith, you aren't going to get anything." Then why even go to church? However, if they had had faith, then they would have been healed. Do you see what I am saying? That was the mental process, and that's what made it so wrong. It put people under condemnation rather than lifting them to get them to walk in the truth and to get help when they needed it. Anything that keeps you from getting help when you need it is not of God. God wants you to get help.

He wants you to get help first from His own Spirit in you; that would be the best way. However, if you are not able to do that, for whatever reason, then get help from the Body of Christ. If you can't get help from the Body of Christ, and if you need to go outside of it, then so be it. I am not against doctors or any of that kind of thing, by any stretch. Get help; alleviate the suffering, especially when it comes to children. They can't tell you how much it hurts. You should never make them suffer for your lack of faith. At the same time, God should be our first resort, not our last resort.

Let's look at this: these people thought they had faith and were telling other people, "I've got faith, but you don't have faith." He was saying, "I am talking to everyone there. I *say* to every man that is among you, not to think of himself more highly than he ought to think. Just because your faith worked for you and their faith didn't work for them, don't make a big deal out of it. Don't think you are better than they are or think more highly of yourself." In other words, "Think soberly; think with a clear-mind."

He said, "According as God has dealt to every man," every person, "*the* measure of faith." Notice it does not say, "He has given to some people a great measure of faith, and to other people a small measure of faith." It doesn't say that at all. It says, "God has dealt to every person *the* measure of faith." If you look *the* measure of faith up in the Greek, a particular, definite article is there. He has given you *the* measure. We all start with the same degree of faith.

Unless there is a genetic issue, we all start with the same number of muscles. We all know that everybody's muscles aren't the same, because some people exercise them and some don't.

We all start with the same measure of faith, but our faith can increase or it can even decrease. It says: "According as God has dealt to every man *the* measure of faith." You have to realize that you don't have *a* measure; you have *the* measure.

You can't say, "Well, I don't have enough faith," because you have been given _the_ measure of faith. The smallest measure of faith that is mentioned in the Bible is faith the size of a grain of mustard seed. Jesus said that faith that size will move a mountain. If you have the smallest amount of faith mentioned, you can move the biggest object in your path.

You could ask, "Then why would I want to grow in faith?" Why would you not want to grow in faith? Secondly, you could ask, "What greater things can I do, then?" It's not so that you can do greater things. It's so that you can have a deeper faith in God. You have a deeper relationship, in faith, with Him.

How big is the measure of faith? It is the smallest measure given in the Bible. If you go from the size of a grain of mustard seed to one step below that, there is no faith. We know that we have faith at least the size of a grain of mustard seed to begin with.

About the measure of faith, He said, "Verily I say unto you, if you have faith as a grain of mustard seed, you shall say unto this mountain remove hence onto yonder place, and nothing shall be impossible unto you." Do you realize that the faith you had the minute you got born again is enough to make it so that nothing shall be impossible to you? Remove the things that you think are going to be impossible to you.

Start removing those things with the faith that's been given to you. It's the gift of God, not of your own, lest you should boast. This faith is the gift of God, and you got that faith the minute you were born again.

Ephesians 2:8-9,

> 8 For by grace are ye saved through faith; and that not of yourselves: it is the gift of God:

> 9 Not of works, lest any man should boast.

The rest of your life is not about you trying to build up this huge amount of faith. It is simply that you are eliminating things that you used to think were impossible. Now you are finding out that they are possible.

Most people believe that God can do anything; they just don't believe He can do *this* thing. It's really easy to believe in general, but it's a whole lot harder to pinpoint it. If you go to a large crowd and you say, "There is someone here with a back problem," that's easy to say. However, if you walk up to a perfect stranger in a mall and say, "Excuse me, but you are having a back problem on your left side, right here," it takes a little bit more boldness and courage. It's easy to believe that God can do anything, but it usually takes a little bit more to believe that He can do *this* thing.

What is the greatest miracle that can ever happen? If I asked you that, you would say, "It is a person being born again; it is salvation." I would then ask you if you believe that, or if you were just sounding religious and saying it to agree with what everybody else says. Is it the greatest miracle?

I'm not putting down other miracles, but I am asking, "Is it the absolute, without a doubt, greatest miracle, that a person can get born again?" That miracle is the new birth, salvation. Are you convinced?

If you were to ask, "How do I get saved?" I would tell you that you get saved by faith. If you are saved, then you have already experienced the greatest miracle that can ever happen. Everything else is downhill from there.

Other miracles might be exciting to watch. For example: if you came across a bus wreck and there were 30 people dead and you got them all to rise from the dead, that would really be neat to watch. However, that still would not be the greatest miracle you have ever experienced.

The greatest miracle you will ever experience is to be born again. How did you get born again? By faith. You have already experienced the greatest miracle by faith, so anything else ought to be easy. You should be able to say, "Oh yes, God can do that." If you tell me, "I don't know if I have enough faith for that. That's awfully big," that tells me that you are looking at it through your eyes and not through God's eyes. To God no problem is big.

Acts 4:12,

> *12 Neither is there salvation in any other: for there is none other name under heaven given among men, whereby we must be saved.*

There is only one Name under heaven whereby men must be saved. It is the name of Jesus and faith in that Name. Faith in that Name got you saved. It raised the lame man in Acts chapter 3. It was the name of Jesus and faith in that Name that made that man stand strong, as Peter said, "In the midst of you all."

I want you to think about this: you have changed your eternal destiny by two things. One is that you *believed* and the second is that you *said*.

You *believe* with the heart and *say* with the confession of the lips. You get born again. You *believe* and you *speak.* "I *believe* therefore I have *spoken.*" This changed your eternal destiny. Now, if that can change your eternal destiny, what do you think it can do with temporal things? What do you think it can do with your temporal body?

If you *believe* and you *speak,* it can fix anything. If it can do the greatest, it stands to reason that it can do anything less. We would say that healing would be less than salvation, in the sense of what's most important in spirit, soul, and body. If that's true, then you have already experienced the greatest thing.

It ought to be an easy thing for you to be able to trust God, who has never lied, who keeps His promises, and somebody you can have faith in. It ought to be easy for you to trust Him to fix your body. You have already done the most impossible thing ever.

However, here is the question: can a leopard change its spots? This is a question that the Bible asks in the Old Testament.

Jeremiah 13:23,

> *23 Can the Ethiopian change his skin, or the leopard his spots? then may ye also do good, that are accustomed to do evil.*

Technically, the leopard can't; that would be impossible. However, the fact is, according to God and according to the new birth, leopards have changed their spots (figuratively speaking). Because of salvation, nothing is impossible. You can change.

People say all the time, "Well, I just can't help it. This is the way I am." Then change. "Well, you don't understand. I can't help it." No, you don't understand. You can help it, because with God, nothing is impossible.

Don't tell me that you can't. When you tell me that you can't, all you are saying is that you don't trust God, you don't believe God, and you don't believe what He said. He said, "Nothing is impossible," and you are saying that you have found something that God can't do. That would make you bigger than God, and you are not bigger than God.

People say, "Yes, He changed me; He recreated me." That's true, but who do you think does healings? People say, "Well, that's God. You can't ever compare salvation with a healing miracle because God changed me and made me a new person." Who do you think raises the dead? Do you think it's you? Of course it's not you. You are just the vessel; you are just the conduit, and you just happen to be there. You believe Him, but it is God who does the works.

There isn't a person who has ever healed a body, healed a bone, or healed a sickness or disease. None of us have ever done any of that. Jesus Himself told us who does the works.

John 14:10,

> *14 Believest thou not that I am in the Father, and the Father in me? the words that I speak unto you I speak not of myself: but the Father that dwelleth in me, he doeth the works.*

Even Jesus didn't take credit for healing the sick. He said, ""It is the Spirit of my Father in Me; He does the works. It has nothing to do with you *per se*, other than the fact that you believe in God, and you have faith in Him.

Is God able? Yes. Is He willing? Yes. Then it should happen. That is how you got born again. Does God want you saved? Yes. Is He able to save you? Yes. If you accept Him and make Him your Lord, then you are born again.

It's easy to heal the sick, raise the dead, cast out devils, preach the Gospel, or anything else you think is impossible. Why? It's because He is still working in and through you. None of us are healing the sick. It's the Spirit of God *in* us that does it.

If the Spirit of God *in* you can heal the sick, then if you get sick, He can heal you by His Spirit that is *in* you. Nothing shall be impossible unto you. You have got to get that; you've got to drill that into yourself.

There are going to be people coming here, and their lives will depend upon you being able to believe that. They are going to come with things that you've never heard of. They are going to come to you with problems that you didn't even know existed. They are going to come to you, and they will need your help, right then. If they ask you to help them and you say, "Oh, yeah, that's tough," right then you can watch them deflate and give up hope. Their hope should be in God, and you represent God to them, so their hope is in you. If they don't see you full of hope and faith, then they will they give up, fall apart, and die.

You are going to be here, and people are going to come in those doors. They are going to talk to you because you come here. You're a member here or you are here regularly, and they know that you've heard this. Even if they are watching by internet, they are saying: "Those people there can help me," because I brag on my people all over the world. Everywhere I go, I brag on you. God gave me a group of people who are spiritually mature that I don't have to babysit all the time. I am blessed. As a result of my bragging on you, and because I go around the world and talk about you, guess what? They are going to come and say, "You are a member of this church; you can do it."

The Tsunami of 2004 occurred on the 26th of December. My son, John, his wife, Stephanie, and my grandson, Josiah, who was two years old at the time, had already bought their tickets to Thailand before the tsunami occurred. They had decided to live there as missionaries. They went over there the last week of 2004. I woke up the morning that it hit, and immediately, I bought tickets for my daughter, Rebekah, and myself. We went to help in the tsunami relief, and arrived within 48 hours after my son and his family had landed.

We were there for about two weeks ministering, setting people free, and getting people born again. We actually started churches in people's homes. Buddhists were getting saved. They kept asking, "What have we done? Is this karma? What have we done to deserve this?" We told them, "You haven't done anything to deserve this; this is the devil. God did not do this to you. The devil is trying to destroy your life, and God sent us here to help you." We got people saved and started home fellowships right there where they were.

People got healed, and blind eyes were opened. Amazing things happened in the midst of all of that. There were dead bodies still in the trees, and they were retrieving them. It was a horrible, horrible situation. We ministered to them, prayed for them, and watched God heal people, and then Rebekah and I left.

As soon as we left, the first thing they did was come to my son and say, "Where's your Dad?" My son said, "He left." They said to him, "Well, here they are, and they are sick; fix them." My son said, "Well, what do you mean?" They said, "You are his son; you know how to do this. Do it!"

My son said, "I had no option. I had to do it." He tried to say, "I'm his son, but I'm not my Dad." However, since it was the same Spirit of God, John started ministering to them, and people started getting healed.

There were certain things happening and John said, "I caught myself saying things I had heard you say, but this time I understood why you said them." He stepped up, even though he didn't understand them beforehand. There are some things you will never learn until you do them. Some revelation does not come until you step out and have to have it in order to help somebody else.

He saw all kinds of amazing things happen over there. I could go into many details and testimonies. We went back over later and saw more things happen, and it was amazing. The reason I am telling you this is because it is the Spirit of God in people; it's not the people. It's not me; it's not John. It wasn't John Lake or Smith Wigglesworth. It's the Spirit of God in people; God does the work. You just have to be able to have faith in Him. Why do you have faith in God? It is because He keeps His promises.

He said, "If you believe and lay hands on the sick, they shall recover." You have to believe that, stand on that, and even if they don't look like they are recovering, you have to believe Him until they do. Somebody has got to trust Him. Somebody has got to have faith in Him.

Say this with me: "Nothing is impossible to me, because I am *in* Him, and all things are possible with Him." Do you believe that? He's *in* you, you're *in* Him, and if nothing is impossible with Him, then nothing is impossible with you.

It's time to do some exploits of faith in God. If you go back to Psalms, it says over and over again how God did these mighty works for Israel and how many times they forgot God.

Psalm 78:4,

> 4 *We will not hide them from their children, shewing to the generation to come the praises of the LORD, and his strength, and his wonderful works that he hath done.*

In other words, "We will not be like those who forgot. We will tell the mighty works of God to our children, and to our children's children, and even to generations that are not yet born. We will tell of the mighty works of God."

During the '40s, '50s, and early '60s, we had this massive Voice of Healing revival start up, and for the first time, healing services were being broadcast right into people's homes. Sometimes they were live and were broadcast right from the studio, and sometimes they were recorded and sent in. They were on television every week.

You could see Jack Coe, A.A. Allen, Oral Roberts, and all of these ministers doing these amazing things by the Spirit of God working through them. They were showing it to the current generation, and there was a great move of God. However, right after that, it was as if they forgot. As soon as they went off after the television aspect of it, they forget to tell the next generation.

Think about this: it was the generation of the '40s, '50s, and going into the '60s. Their kids were the ones in the '60s who took up with the hippie movement, the drugs, the experimentation, and all of that. Why did they go into those things? It was because they did not see the reality of God's power in their lives, even though they had heard about it.

They didn't see it in their families, they didn't see it in their churches, and they didn't see it amongst their own selves. They started looking at other things. They started looking at eastern philosophy and eastern religions. They started going into drugs and everything else.

There was this really good chance for America to hit a spiritually high level and to literally become great all over again by infecting the rest of the world with the Gospel of Jesus Christ.

There is an aspect of this that we have to carry on to the next generation. We have to believe it, and we have to live it. It is time for God to do exploits again, through us, and let the people of the world see that God is in the Church.

We know that faith can fluctuate. Let's prove that. Go back to Matthew chapter10.

Matthew 10:1, 7-8,

> *1 And when he had called unto him his twelve disciples, he gave them power against unclean spirits, to cast them out, and to heal all manner of sickness and all manner of disease.*

> *7 And as ye go, preach, saying, The kingdom of heaven is at hand.*

> *8 Heal the sick, cleanse the lepers, raise the dead, cast out devils: freely ye have received, freely give.*

What did the disciples do? They went out, healed the sick, and cast out devils; they did all of that. They came back rejoicing, because the devils were subject to them. Jesus said, "Don't rejoice over power, but that your names are written in heaven." We know that they accomplished great things. We know they had faith in God to do these things, because they did them.

The disciples had already been out casting out devils and healing the sick. They returned excited; we know that. However, in Matthew 17, after they had been out doing that, they came across this one boy who had what we would today call an epileptic seizure. They said it was a demon, and Jesus cast the thing out.

The disciples couldn't get that out of that boy, so obviously their faith had fluctuated. They asked, "Why couldn't we do it?" Jesus said, "It was because of your unbelief." They had already done it before, but then they moved into unbelief. We don't want to be like that. We don't want to see God do things, then move into unbelief and always be talking about yesterday.

Let's look at a manifestation of the *spirit of faith*. How does the *spirit of faith* manifest in your daily life? What would be a synonym or description of the *spirit of faith*? It would be expectancy.

Are you expecting God to do something on a daily basis? Do you have an expectation of God to do something through you? Are you open to it? Are you looking for it, or do you have tunnel vision? Are you just in your little world, busy doing your own thing, or are you really walking with God? As you go, are you looking for God to use you?

There has to be an expectation with anticipation and joy. In your daily life, do you wake up in the morning with joy? When I get up in the morning, I am ready to go. I am excited to see what God is going to do that day. Whether it is through me or somebody else, I am excited.

I don't wake up thinking, "Ugh, I've got to go to the office. I've got to go there and do this again." It's not like that at all; I'm excited. You might say, "Yes, but you have a cool job – look at what you are doing, look at what you are hearing, and look at what you are seeing." You are supposed to be doing exactly what I am doing, except for the fact that you've got somebody else paying you. God uses your job to pay you to do His work. That's smart.

You say, "Well, I can't really preach because if I do, I will get fired." Okay then, get fired. Come in here, and we'll let you testify that you got fired for preaching. Then, somebody will hear you and say, "Hey, I've got a job for you." It will be better than the one you lost.

You have to have joy, excitement, and optimism, and you have to be ready to take risks. You have to be looking for something to use your faith on, and you have to step out into exploits. That is how the *spirit of faith* manifests in a person's life. You have got to be looking.

One time, after we had just started this one thing, I told my wife that we needed to do this other thing. She told me, "Well, Curry, you can't do everything," and I said, "Why not? Who says we can't? Let's move into this; it needs to be done."

You use your faith to get it going. Once it is going and you realize that you can step back and it will keep running, then it is time to find something else to put your faith on. You can't just let your faith sit around; you keep it busy.

Jesus said that faith is your servant. He said, "Which of you, having a servant, goes out into the field and comes back and says, 'Sit down and let me cook for you'? No, instead he would say, 'You've got one more job to do: cook and feed me. Then, after that, you can eat.'" This is from Luke 17:7-9. He was talking about faith. He was saying that your faith should be working for you.

We shouldn't sit and talk about the laurels of yesterday, or about the time we saw the dead raised, or about when we saw the sick healed. No, it should be today. Your faith should always be working. You ought to always be finding something to put your faith on. The *spirit of faith* makes you want to do that.

Ephesians 2:10,

10 For we are his workmanship, created in Christ Jesus unto good works, which God hath before ordained that we should walk in them.

"For we are His workmanship…" Think about that. He created you, He built you, and He made you, so you must have some type of potential. You are not who you think you are; you are who He says you are. It says: "For we are His workmanship, created in Christ Jesus unto good works." You are created for what? "Unto good works." Do you hear that? You were created for good works. You weren't created to sit around, twiddle your thumbs, and hope to someday be whisked out of here.

Don't say, "Well, I'm just waiting until the end. I'm waiting until I can step over to the other side." Get some things done before you step over to the other side. Don't just be waiting for quitting time. Have you ever seen those employees who stand with their card in their hands just waiting to punch out? "Click! I'm out of here." You won't last long living like that around here or for the Kingdom of God. Why? There's too much to do.

It says: "Created in Christ Jesus unto good works, which God has before ordained that we should walk in them." There are people out there who are your good works. They are walking around sick, hurting, dying, and waiting. They are your good works that God is waiting for you to get to: "Which God hath before ordained that we should walk in them." He has already foreordained that you are to be the one to lay hands on them.

If you won't do your job, He will find somebody else who will. However, He has already ordained that you should do it. He's got testimonies out there waiting for you to come and fulfill. He has provided them for you. He gave you devils to beat up, just to practice on. Listen: these people that we have seen healed are trophies that we lay at Jesus' feet. These are those crowns that you are able to throw at His feet and say, "All of this is for You."

We have to realize that we aren't going to be able stand there and say, "This is what I've done." We have to be able to say, "This is what I have done for You, because I love You. I can't show You how much I love You except that I show it to people. As I show people how much I love You, by loving them and setting them free, then they will know Your love, and they will come to You." That is how you do that.

The cancer that I drive out of that person is an enemy that God is waiting for me to make His footstool. God is waiting for you to drive out that sickness, disease, or whatever it is and make it His footstool.

Hebrews 10:12-13,

> *12 But this man, after he had offered one sacrifice for sins for ever, sat down on the right hand of God;*

> *13 From henceforth expecting till his enemies be made his footstool.*

Jesus is seated, waiting "until His enemies be made His footstool." Jesus is seated, waiting until His enemies be made His footstool. He's already defeated them, and He is already seated, so we know it wasn't Him defeating them at the cross that made them His footstool. He is still waiting "until his enemies be made His footstool." Who is going to make them His footstool? His Body is going to do that. You are His Body. You need to realize that.

Romans 8:19-22,

> *19 For the earnest expectation of the creature waiteth for the manifestation of the sons of God.*

20 For the creature was made subject to vanity, not willingly, but by reason of him who hath subjected the same in hope,

21 Because the creature itself also shall be delivered from the bondage of corruption into the glorious liberty of the children of God.

22 For we know that the whole creation groaneth and travaileth in pain together until now.

He is seated, waiting for the manifestation of the sons of God, just like the world is groaning, waiting for us to grow up and show up. The world is waiting for us to manifest; God is waiting for us to manifest.

We always talk about devils manifesting and say, "Oh, did you see that devil manifesting?" It's always a big deal. How do we know it manifested? It did something that drew attention. It says here: "The whole world is waiting for the sons of God to manifest." What does that mean? It means that we are going to show up and do something that draws some attention. As soon as that attention comes to us, we are going to redirect it and say, "That was Him."

You can like it or not like it; I don't care. If you like it, it was still Him. If you don't like it, it was still Him. Why? It's because it's not me that does it; it's my Father *in* me, and He does the works. If you don't like what I do, don't talk to me about it; talk to Him about it. Talk Him into firing me and I will sit around and write books. I wouldn't have to be nearly as busy.

We talk about demons manifesting, but it's time for sons to manifest.

When you look at a person and see a demon manifest, you command it to stop, and it stops. We need to go to places like emergency rooms in the hospital. We need to go to malls and places where you see lots of people. We need to be able to say, "I don't want to embarrass you, but I think I am fixing to manifest. I just feel a manifestation coming on. I'm telling you, I'm fixing to start laying hands on the sick, and I'm fixing to start casting out devils. If you don't want to be embarrassed, you might want to step aside. I just feel a manifestation coming on. I can tell it, and I am just giving you fair warning." Then, just go and manifest.

People will ask, "What was that?" and you will say, "I'm sorry; I was just manifesting. I was just filled with anger at that sickness. I was controlled and influenced by the Spirit of God and His attitude toward that cancer. I apologize for the way I did it, but I don't apologize for the fact that I did it."

Have you ever gone somewhere with a child and wondered what they were going to say? You never know what they are going to say or do. Art Linkletter made a career out of children saying things that were not expected. You know that whatever they say, they are going to say the wrong thing at the wrong time.

You can raise a child holy and teach them everything just right, and they will go to a friend's house, one time, watch a movie that has one bad word in it, and everywhere you take them from then on, at some point, that word will come out. Have you ever noticed that? You say, "He didn't get that from me. He got that from the neighbor." It will always come out when it shouldn't. Why? It's because kids don't think the way we do. It just comes out, and they just act.

Do you ever wonder why Jesus said, "You must become as a little child?" Your problem is that you think too much. You look at a situation and you say, "Oh, that person needs help." However, instead of going to help them, you say, "If I go and do this and it doesn't work, then this will happen; I will be embarrassed, and it will bring disrepute on God." You talk yourself out of it.

You may have a child with you, and if the child has been raised right, the child will walk right over there, lay hands on them, and command that they be healed while you are sitting there thinking about it. The whole time you will be thinking, "I hope he didn't embarrass that person." The person will say, "I'm healed." Then you will say, "That's my boy! I raised him!"

It's always right to do the right thing. As it says, in Philippians 4:13, "I can do all things through Christ who strengthens me." The people who know their God shall be strong and do exploits. It's time to do some exploits. You have got to make a choice to do exploits.

I am going to show you about some exploits and how the *spirit of faith* was manifested.

Hebrews chapter 11:

> 4 *By faith Abel offered unto God a more excellent sacrifice than Cain, by which he obtained witness that he was righteous, God testifying of his gifts: and by it he being dead yet speaketh.*

> 7 *By faith Noah, being warned of God of things not seen as yet, moved with fear, prepared an ark to the saving of his house; by the which he condemned the world, and became heir of the righteousness which is by faith.*

8 <u>By faith</u> Abraham, when he was called to go out into a place which he should after receive for an inheritance, <u>obeyed</u>; and he went out, not knowing whither he went.

11 <u>Through faith</u> also Sara herself <u>received strength to conceive seed</u>, and was delivered of a child when she was past age, because she judged him faithful who had promised.

24 <u>By faith</u> Moses, when he was come to years, <u>refused to be called the son of Pharaoh's daughter;</u>

25 <u>Choosing rather to suffer affliction</u> with the people of God, <u>than to enjoy the pleasures of sin for a season;</u>

29 <u>By faith</u> they <u>passed through the Red sea as by dry land</u>: which the Egyptians assaying to do were drowned.

30 <u>By faith the walls of Jericho fell down</u>, after they were compassed about seven days.

Hebrews 11:4: the *spirit of faith* offers a more excellent sacrifice. Hebrews 11:7: the *spirit of faith* prepared an ark. Hebrews 11:8: the *spirit of faith* obeyed, went out, not knowing where he went.

If you will notice, I am taking out the names because we are to follow their faith and do what they did. You can put your own name in there, because they all did it by faith. Everyone in Hebrews 11 did what they did by faith; they chose to believe God. You can choose to believe God, so all of these exploits are what you could have done, had you been there and had chosen to believe God. The name on it does not matter, because all of it was the Spirit of God working through them.

Hebrews 11:11: the *spirit of faith* receives strength to conceive a child. Hebrews 11:24-25: the *spirit of faith* refused to identify with Egypt, even though it meant suffering. Hebrews 11:29: the *spirit of faith* caused the Israelites to pass through the Red Sea as by dry land. They had to have faith to walk across that dry ground. Hebrews 11:30: the *spirit of faith* caused the walls of Jericho to fall down.

> *32 And what shall I more say? for the time would fail me to tell of Gedeon, and of Barak, and of Samson, and of Jephthae; of David also, and Samuel, and of the prophets:*

> *33 Who through faith subdued kingdoms, wrought righteousness, obtained promises, stopped the mouths of lions,*

34 Quenched the violence of fire, escaped the edge of the sword, out of weakness were made strong, waxed valiant in fight, turned to flight the armies of the aliens.

35 Women received their dead raised to life again: and others were tortured, not accepting deliverance; that they might obtain a better resurrection:

36 And others had trial of cruel mockings and scourgings, yea, moreover of bonds and imprisonment:

37 They were stoned, they were sawn asunder, were tempted, were slain with the sword: they wandered about in sheepskins and goatskins; being destitute, afflicted, tormented;

Look at Hebrews 11:32: "And what shall I more say? For the time would fail me to tell of Gedeon, and of Barak, and of Samson, and of Jephthae; of David also, and Samuel, and of the prophets." Notice: it doesn't say they did it through an anointing, a gifting, or through a special calling.

Of every one of these it says: "Who through faith subdued kingdoms, worked righteousness, obtained promises, stopped the mouths of lions, quenched the violence of fire, escaped the edge of the sword, out of weakness were made strong, waxed valiant in fight, and turned to flight the armies of the aliens. Women received their dead raised to life again." How? By faith. It says, "And others were tortured, not accepting deliverance." It goes on: "That they might obtain a better resurrection: and others had trial of cruel mockings and scourgings, yea, moreover of bonds and imprisonment: they were stoned, they were sawn asunder, were tempted, were slain with the sword: they wandered about in sheepskins and goatskins; being destitute, afflicted, and tormented."

God's opinion of them is in Hebrews 11:38:

> *38 (Of whom the world was not worthy:) they wandered in deserts, and in mountains, and in dens and caves of the earth.*
>
> *39 And these all, having obtained a good report through faith, received not the promise:*
>
> *40 God having provided some better thing for us, that they without us should not be made perfect.*

"Of whom the world was not worthy." Why? That was because they did what they did by faith. Faith gave them a standing, a stature in God's eyes, to where God said the world didn't deserve them. Think about that. That's who you want to be. You want God to say, "The world doesn't deserve you." Why? It's because you trust in Him, and you do exploits.

In Hebrews 11:39-41, it tells us: "They wandered in deserts, and in mountains, and in dens, and caves of the earth. And these all, having obtained a good report through faith, received not the promise: God having provided some better thing for us." In the midst of all of these things, God says that He has provided some better things for us, "That they without us should not be made perfect." In other words, they did all of these things; they had all of their faith in God, yet they were still waiting until this time. They were waiting for us.

Hebrews 12:1-2,

> *1 Wherefore seeing we also are compassed about with so great a cloud of witnesses, let us lay aside every weight, and the sin which doth so easily beset us, and let us run with patience the race that is set before us,*

> *2 Looking unto Jesus the author and finisher of our faith; who for the joy that was set before him endured the cross, despising the shame, and is set down at the right hand of the throne of God.*

It says, "Wherefore seeing (knowing or perceiving) we also are compassed about with so great a cloud of witnesses." What is this great cloud of witnesses that he was talking about?

First of all, he didn't say that they are in heaven looking down on us. It does not say that they look over the balcony of heaven and see us.

It says, "Wherefore seeing (knowing or perceiving) we also are compassed about with so great a cloud of witnesses." What is this great cloud of witnesses that he was talking about?

It says, "We are *compassed about...*" What does *compassed about* mean? It means: *they surround us.* If your loved ones died in faith, they are not at some distance; they are right there. As a matter of fact, if they made it, they are saying, "We made it. It's worth it. Come on; go for it. Go all out. Don't back off, and don't back down. Don't try to put it on cruise control and just coast through. If you knew what was over here, you would be running as hard as you can, because it's worth it."

I've got friends in that great cloud of witnesses now. They are men of God, family members, and different people. I am telling you that they are right there. They are not in some far-off distance. They are right there, urging us on and saying, "You can do this. It's worth it. I know what God has put in you. You can do this."

We are compassed about by angels. We have a great cloud of *witnesses*. The word w*itnesses* actually means *martyrs*. We are *compassed about* by a great cloud of *martyrs,* people who have died for the faith and who died as witnesses. Think about that. You are *compassed about* by angels and witnesses.

You need to get your eyes off this temporal world, and quit thinking about the temporal side. Realize what is eternal, and how good the eternal is. It is the next dimension; one could say, "The spiritual realm." Walk and live there.

Many times, just before people actually pass away, they are in this in-between state. They talk about things that they see in the spirit realm.

There is a movie out right now, and it's called *Lone Survivor.* It's about Operation Red Wing, which was about four Navy Seals who went into Afghanistan and ended up getting caught there. Three of them died there, but one made it out. Marcus Luttrell made it out, and he told his story.

One of the Navy Seals who died there was named Michael Murphy. I have the video documentary about him, and it's called *Murph the Protector*. Being the protector was his whole attitude. He was always being sent on deployments, but he wouldn't talk about what happened over there.

He said, "When I leave, I don't say goodbye. I say, 'See you later.'" The last time his Mom saw him she turned to him and said, "Goodbye." He said, "Mom, it is not goodbye. It is 'See you later.'" She said, "Oh, yes, don't pay any attention to me. That's right." However, it was the last time she ever saw him.

He was supposed to go to Hawaii, but instead he was redirected to Afghanistan. She had told him before he left, "When you get to Hawaii, send us a text to let us know you made it there safely." They were waiting, but they never got the text. They tried to call him but couldn't ever reach him. He had been deployed and sent to Afghanistan. He was killed around the 4th of July. They brought his body back to Dover Air Force Base, and his family was there.

They watched the casket come down, and the Honor Guard was there to pick up the casket. His mom said that when his casket came down, it was like she saw him. She said, "It was like he got up and started walking toward us. He was in his dress whites, and he was really bright as he walked toward us." She said, "About the time that he got to me, it was the strangest thing, because I felt his presence and his warmth, like he hugged me." She said, "I felt warmth around my arms, like where his arms would be." She said that he hugged her, and then he went back to the casket. I am just telling you what she said. Then, they went to the funeral.

After the funeral, they took the wreaths and put them on the gravesite. The car that they were going to ride back in was 50 feet away from his Mom and Dad. As they turned to walk back, within that 50 foot space, her phone started ringing. She thought, "Who is calling me? I told everyone we were going to be at the funeral." She pulled out her phone, looked at it, and then her knees buckled; she almost went down. At that point, his Dad asked, "What's wrong?" She handed the phone to his Dad. She had received a text from him saying: "Mom, I'm home safe."

I have no theology to explain all of that, but I know this – God is good. He loves us. He loves you; He loves every aspect of you. He knows what's going on. However He made that text come through, two or three months later, it was the grace and goodness of God.

She said that from that time on, she never cried until they started making the documentary. They started making her relive it all. The only reason I brought this up is that I want you to realize (pro or con, for or against the war), "Greater love hath no man, than this: that he would lay down his life for a friend." If you listen to his life story, it is amazing. He was a Christian. He had confessed Christ as his Lord and Savior.

I could give you many other stories like this. I know that when my first daughter passed away, my parents came up for the funeral, and they were staying at a hotel up in Sherman. My Mom woke up and said that Erika was standing at the foot of the bed. She could see her as clear as day and all she said was, "Grandma, I am okay, and I am happy." She was only two years, two months, and 23 days when she passed.

We are *compassed about* (surrounded) by a great cloud of witnesses. They are not far off; they are just in the next dimension. They are in that spirit realm. They are watching, and if you could hear them, they would be saying, "Go for it! Run all out!"

Many times, when someone is running and they stumble, it is because they start looking around instead of keeping their eye on the finish line and staying focused. If they start to slow down, goof off, or start showboating, that is when they drop the baton, stumble, and fall.

The key to walking in faith and the key to manifesting the *spirit of faith* is very simply this: give 100 percent, all out, nothing barred. When I say, "All out," I mean to go for it completely; push and run; don't hesitate. Don't think about what people think, and don't think about what people are going to say about you. You just go all out. You get out of yourself. You forget about yourself, and just do what you are supposed to do. You won't care how it looks; just go all out.

Let's go back to what it said in Hebrews chapter 12.

> *1 Wherefore seeing we also are compassed about with so great a cloud of witnesses, let us lay aside every weight, and the sin which doth so easily beset us, and let us run with patience the race that is set before us,*

The word *patience* means *consistent endurance.* They have already run the race. It should be easier for us. Everything is easier after you see someone else do it. It ought to be easy to heal the sick. It ought to be easy to raise the dead. It ought to be easy to preach the Gospel. Why? It's because you have seen other people do it.

That is the *why* of discipleship. Discipleship is when you watch somebody else do it, and it makes it easier for you to do it. That's why the devil has fought discipleship so much.

> 2 *Looking unto Jesus the author and finisher of our faith; who for the joy that was set before him endured the cross, despising the shame, and is set down at the right hand of the throne of God.*

"Looking unto Jesus the author and finisher of our faith…" I will give you two names of people who manifested the *spirit of faith*.

John Lake is one, and I could tell you stories of how he did it, but needless to say, he had 100,000 healings in Spokane. He also had 100,000 healings in Portland. With the *spirit of faith* in him, he boldly stepped out causing a revival in Africa that is still affecting Africa. It was the *spirit of faith* in him.

Another person who had the *spirit of faith* was George Mueller. George Mueller raised, housed, and fed thousands of orphans. George Mueller raised, housed, and fed thousands of orphans. Millions of dollars went through his hands, although he had said that he would never ask a person for money. Let me just read this last part of what was written about him to you:

"George Mueller did not believe he had any special gift of faith. To the contrary, he stated emphatically that the faith he operated in was the same simple faith that any child of God possessed and not anything special."

When he started the orphanages, he said that he did it for three reasons:

1. We are doing this so people will see that God answers prayer and that God may be glorified.

2. We are doing this so the faith of His children will be strengthened.

3. We are doing this so people can see that God can be trusted.

He said, "We are starting the orphanages so that God may be glorified. Should He be pleased to furnish me with the means, in it being seen that it is not a vain thing to trust Him, and thus the faith of His children will be strengthened." In other words, "We're doing this so people will see that God answers prayer. We are doing this so that God's children and their faith will be strengthened. We are doing this so people can see that God can be trusted." Think about that. It was an exploit of faith. Out of that came over 10,000 orphans over a period of time. Millions of dollars were spent, and he never asked for a dime.

You may have heard the stories. They would get up in the morning with no food. The helpers would come in and say, "We don't have any food for the kids." He would say, "Take them into the dining area, sit them down, set the table, get ready, and we will pray." He would start praying and somebody would be knocking at the door saying, "Brother Mueller, last night I could not sleep. I know you need some bread, so I baked all of this bread. It's more than I can use. I know you need it. Here it is."

They brought in the bread, but they still needed other food, so they started praying. The wagon that carried the other food broke an axle in front of their house. They said, "We can't move the thing, and we can't fix it until we unload all of this food. If we wait that long to reload it and take it back, it will ruin. Do you here at the orphanage by any chance need 5,000 pounds of fruits and vegetables?" He told them, "Bring it on in." God answered his prayers.

He was manifesting the *spirit of faith*, the same *spirit of faith* that you have.

If I can just get that into you, you can do exploits by the *spirit of faith,* having faith in God because you know that He can be trusted and because He keeps His promises.

If I can just get that into you, you can do exploits by the *spirit of faith*. You have faith in God because you know that He can be trusted and because He keeps His promises.

I am glad that we made the decision long ago to keep going with the ministry. Like I said before, "I am not going to turn 70, sitting on my front porch in a rocking chair wondering, 'What if?' I had rather try and fail miserably, and then, get on with my life and forget all of this faith business, if it's not real."

We stepped out, we took risks, and God has met us all along the way. We now have influence, literally, on every continent. We are seeing so many people healed, delivered, and set free. Why? It's because we manifest the *spirit of faith*. We chose to do it.

It is our choice to bring trophies to God, on purpose, to say, "You are God, and you deserve it. The people of God need to have their faith strengthened. The world needs to know there is a God and that He answers prayer." We made that decision, and we haven't stopped. As a matter of fact, even with all we've done, we haven't even gotten started yet.

They told Dr. Sumrall, "Sumrall, you're 50, and you're finished." He said, "Well, in a couple of months I will be 55, and I haven't even begun yet." Amen?

This is all just a warm-up. I want you to watch what God is going to do. I refuse to get on cruise control and just cruise through life. I refuse. I want to stretch.

That's why I hang out with people like David Hogan; he stretches me. He makes me want to do more for God. We bring him in here so that he will infect you and get you wanting to do more for God. It's about getting you bold so you will step out and do exploits. There will be things that people tell you that you can't do. I am telling you that God, through you, can do them.

Let us pray,

"In the name of Jesus, your needs are met by Jesus Christ. By His Spirit, you are healed. You are whole. You are made free. As a matter of fact, if you are not born again, just receive Him, and everything He has just moves into you with Him. He brings all things with Him.

"He brings healing. He brings deliverance. He brings freedom. He brings joy, peace, long-suffering, and all of these things. He brings them with Him, and you just receive them.

"The minute you get born again, you get healed. As far as God is concerned it is done, so we set you free in Jesus' name. Amen. Be healed in Jesus' name. I set you free. Jesus did it 2000 years ago. He paid for it, and I am just announcing the decree from the King that He has set you free.

"He has destroyed the works of the devil, and right now, we enforce that victory over His enemy. Sickness, disease, demonic influence, addictions, habits, confusion in the mind, and torment, I command, in the name of Jesus, GO! Set these people free in Jesus' name. You have no place here. In the name of Jesus, so be it. Amen."

Give God glory and begin to thank Him. Jesus Christ makes you whole. Jesus Christ sets you free. So be it. Amen.

- You are left unsatisfied by the status quo...
- You know you were meant to be a participant and not just a spectator...
- You ask "Why not?..." more than "Why?"...
- You believe that today can be better than yesterday...
- You know you were meant to walk among the Giants of the Faith, and you want the tools & training that can make it happen...
- When you hear the exploits of God's Generals, you can picture yourself doing them...

If this describes you, then you ARE JGLM...
whether you know it or not.

COME.
LET'S CHANGE THE WORLD.

John G. Lake Ministries
SAME MESSAGE. SAME POWER. SAME RESULTS.

LIFE TEAM
The Saints Army

lifeteams@jglm.org

Go out into all the world. Preach the gospel, heal the sick, cast out demons and make disciples

DOMINION
BIBLE INSTITUTE
TRAINING THE NEXT GENERATION OF GOD'S GENERALS

SIGN UP TODAY!
dbi@jglm.org

John G. Lake Ministries
SAME MESSAGE. SAME POWER. SAME RESULTS.

John G. Lake Ministries
SAME MESSAGE. SAME POWER. SAME RESULTS.

PARTNER WITH US AS WE ADVANCE GOD'S KINGDOM ON EARTH!

Partner Benefits Include:

- Our monthly "Laboring Together" newsletter with a ministry update directly from Brother Curry that includes detailed information about our upcoming events and activities. We compile testimonies from all over the world to encourage and strengthen your faith.

- Partner E-Newsletter includes an MP3 every month taught by Brother Curry with the option to download our monthly audio teaching.

- 30% Discount on all products during the holiday season...

- Our Promise to Protect Your Kingdom Investment.

Partners can choose to receive packets by postal mail or via email. Your faithful support allows us to help give our materials away freely to those who cannot give, such as our JGLM prison ministries, disaster relief funds and foreign missionaries. Most importantly we depend on our faithful partners as our main line of prayer support.

Email: partners@jglm.org
www.jglm.org/partners

The Teaching That Birthed A Legend
Is Now Raising An Army.

Get Yours Today
Call **888-293-6591**
or Visit Us Online

store.jglm.org

John G. Lake Ministries
SAME MESSAGE. SAME POWER. SAME RESULTS.

New Man

This Changes Everything...

The Primary focus of the DHT seminar is to train believers to biblically and effectively minister healing. The purpose of the New Man seminar is to reveal to believers what was accomplished by Jesus for us through His death, burial, and resurrection. The New Man Seminar reveals what you are (in Christ) not what you will some day become. It also reveals how to begin being who you are rather than emphasizing waiting for the next "Christian Fad".

John G. Lake Ministries
SAME MESSAGE. SAME POWER. SAME RESULTS.

DOMINION LIFE
INTERNATIONAL APOSTOLIC CHURCH

Glory to God, Freedom for All!

Join us online every Sunday at 10am:
broadcast.jglm.org
To learn more about Dominion Life visit:
jglm.org/dominion-life-church
or email: dliac@jglm.org

Church Membership Requirements

1. Must confess Jesus as Lord and that you are saved and born again.

2. Must at least be seeking and expecting to be filled with the Holy Spirit in accordance with Acts Chapter 2 (speaking with other tongues).

3. Must agree with the JGLM/IAC Statement of Faith, obtained by emailing us at: dliac@jglm.org.

4. You agree to pray for us according to the prayer directives that we will send to all church members on a regular basis.

5. You agree to support the church through tithes and offerings. Tithes and offerings must be sent to the church address and MUST be noted as Tithes/Offerings.

6. You agree to work towards becoming a certified DHT. Our hope is that ALL DLIAC members work toward becoming a certified DHT to advance the kingdom through this body. For information on becoming a DHT contact us by email at: iac@jglm.org or you can find all information on our website at www.jglm.org.

7. You agree to remain in the unity of the Spirit by living a life in accordance with the constitution and bylaws of the I.A.C.

John G. Lake Ministries
SAME MESSAGE. SAME POWER. SAME RESULTS.